THE BOOK OF
DAWLISH

• AN HISTORICAL PORTRAIT OF A SEASIDE TOWN •

COMPILED BY

FRANK PEARCE

WITH PHOTOGRAPHS
AND ADDITIONAL INFORMATION FROM
BERNARD CHAPMAN

HALSGROVE

First published in Great Britain in 2001

British Library Cataloguing-in-Publication Data
A CIP record for this title is available from the British Library

ISBN 1 84114 110 0

HALSGROVE
PUBLISHING, MEDIA AND DISTRIBUTION

Halsgrove House
Lower Moor Way
Tiverton, Devon EX16 6SS
Tel: 01884 243242
Fax: 01884 243325
website: http//www.halsgrove.com
email: sales@halsgrove.com

The vignette on the title page shows the first pair of the famous black swans
of Dawlish in 1908. They were given by Mr W. French.

Printed and bound in Great Britain by Bookcraft Ltd, Midsomer Norton

Contents

Acknowledgements

The author and publisher wish to thank all those who have assisted in the compilation of this book. Though too many to name individually, there are those who deserve particular mention. Bernard Chapman, the last of that family to have been directly involved in their photography and postcard business in Dawlish, has been unfailingly generous in allowing the use of the photographs and the notes he appended to them. To him we offer our grateful acknowledgement. Thanks are also due to Muriel Sawtell who provided the extracts from her memoirs.

MURIEL E.B. SAWTELL

Quoted extracts appearing throughout the book come from the memoirs of Muriel Sawtell who spent her childhood days in the town, moving there in 1931 from Exeter when she was five years old. She writes: 'I loved growing up in Dawlish and have so many memories of times and incidents there. My youngest brother, Geoffrey Robins, now 69 years, was born in Riviera Terrace, and has lived in Dawlish all his life.' The publishers express their warm thanks for the use of her work.

Preface
The Chapmans of Dawlish

It is appropriate to preface this book with some information concerning the photographers from whose work the volume is largely drawn. Indeed, its compilation would not have been possible without reference to a series of photograph albums compiled by the last member of the Chapman photography dynasty, Bernard, to whom the author and publisher acknowledge their grateful thanks.

The four principals in the business were W.J. Chapman 1830–1923 (Bernard's great-grandfather), W.S. Chapman 1859–1918 (grandfather), S.W. Chapman 1898–1987 (father), and Bernard himself (1926–).

In an introduction to the four original volumes, Bernard Chapman wrote:

In 1963 the firm of Chapman & Son celebrated one hundred years of existence as a photographic business. Casting around for some means of commemorating a period which was very nearly as long as photography had been known, I thought of recording the past one hundred years of Dawlish history in pictures.

I have always wanted to go back to the middle of the last century with a camera in my hand. These photographs, gathered from many different sources, have been the next best thing. Sometimes

a picture can evoke a sense of period, a grasp of life as it was then, that the written word does not communicate.

In these pages will be found a broad coverage of people, places, and events in Dawlish since 1853, and because this idea grew out of the family business, I thought it only fitting to preface the book with a short résumé of Chapman & Son's progress.

My great-grandfather on my father's side was born in Exeter in 1830 and, when he reached the age for work, became a member of the family dyeing business. An old diary of his shows that in 1859 he received 7s.6d. 'for photography'. In 1863 he came to Dawlish and opened a photography business at the top of Town Tree Hill. Later he moved to 20 Regent Street. In those days Regent Street was a main road and Park Road a minor one.

One of my great-grandfather's sons, my grandfather, joined him in the business. By the 1890s they were running a small industry in plush goods. They consisted mainly of trinket boxes made of cardboard covered in plush, with a photograph of a local scene mounted under the glass for a lid. Space was limited at 20 Regent Street so the works was built at the top of Hatcher Street.

By 1907 the popularity of plush goods was waning but postcards were becoming popular so

A dynasty of Dawlish photography. From left: *W.J. Chapman 1830–1923, W.S. Chapman 1859–1918, S.W. Chapman 1898–1987, and Bernard Chapman (1926–).*

W.J. Chapman, founder of the Dawlish photographic business (centre) surrounded by family members, c.1904.

the business was adapted to their production. To photograph the views great-grandfather and grandfather travelled to the wilds of Dartmoor in a pony and trap, and frequently on foot, carrying their huge and weighty equipment to inaccessible places. Dartmoor was usually reached by train to stations such as Ashburton, Bovey Tracey, Tavistock, Princetown, etc., there to be met by a pre-arranged pony and trap. After World War One my father (S.W.) visited Dartmoor in his own car.

In June 1918 grandfather died suddenly, while great-grandfather was still alive, and my father,

the only son, was in the Navy. Great-grandfather lived on until 1923 when he died aged 93.

When my father was demobilised he joined two of his five sisters, Lilian and Dorothy, in the business. They prospered steadily until the outbreak of World War Two. At this time the restriction of materials made it almost impossible to carry on. My father and mother left Dawlish for war work in a Weston-super-Mare factory, and my two aunts, Lil and Doll, kept the business going.

After the war Lil and Doll decided to dissolve the partnership and leave the business. My father then worked on his own until my demobilisation from the Army in 1948, when a new partnership was formed. For many years Aunt Lil continued to name all the postcard negatives and recorded their addition to our range in a book in which she noted any interesting details of the day, from important events to the state of the weather.

Postcard production continued to total around 29 000. The current series went to Byles of Bristol and the out of date negatives to the Devon Record Office.

The interior of the plush-making works, c.1900.

Chapter 1
Dawlish at the End of the Nineteenth Century

Dawlish seafront from the station, c.1893.

As this book deals largely with the last years of Queen Victoria's reign and continues towards the middle years of the twentieth century, it is appropriate to set the scene in Dawlish around 1900. The following extract from *Black's Guide Book* of 1898 paints an evocative picture of the town:

This favourite sea-side resort, one of the neatest and prettiest in Devon, occupies a cove shut in by honeycombed rocks of deep red sandstone. Through the valley which here opens out upon the sea runs a tamed rivulet, spanned by numerous little bridges, and banked on each side by a broad border of smooth greensward. Along this 'Lawn' stretch inland houses and shops, many of them in their own snug little plots of garden-ground; on the hill-slopes beyond are perched numerous villas, and the cliff front is crowned with terraces looking out to sea. By the 'Strand' and up the valley towards what is called 'Dawlish Water' myrtles, hydrangeas, and other delicate plants bloom freely in a climate which is decidedly mild, not to say relaxing, in summer and autumn, but in the early

part of the year must suffer from east winds. To the south of the town is Lea Mount, a public garden tastefully laid out, and well provided with walks and seats from which to enjoy the views and the contrast of warm red and green displayed by the cliffs.

The only fault to be found with the amenities of Dawlish is the way in which the railway cuts it off from the shore. Passing under the line at the station we find a fine stretch of sand, on which stands a large Ladies' Bathing Pavilion. The gentlemen's bathing place is round the corner under Lea Mount, to which one used to pass through a tunnel, taken away since a fall of rock here caused a fatal accident. At the corner is a little esplanade from which walks have been cut up the cliff. Beyond this there are machines in summer, and hollows in the rock to serve as natural dressing-places.

The Parish Church stands about half a mile up the valley, reached by one very pleasant walk above it to the left. It is a fine rebuilt structure, containing

A view of the lawn, 1913. Children sail their yachts on the pond and the Sea View Restaurant advertises 'chops and steaks at shortest notice; tea and coffee always ready.'

Above: *Newhay Falls, 1900 – just one of the scenic delights awaiting visitors to Dawlish.*

Above right: *The boat cove, c.1900.*

Right: *Boat cove and main beach, c.1875.*

Marine Parade, c.1892. The building in the centre is the Public Baths, built in 1830. Inside bathers had a choice of hot or cold, salt- or fresh-water baths, and hip- or shower-baths. Water was raised from the sea by a large pump. The building was altered in 1895 and later became a gentlemen's club, then a restaurant.

The corner shop in Beach Lane, 1908, and beyond Eveleigh's Railway Inn and the Exeter Inn.

two monuments by Flaxman. Visitors often attend the services at Cofton Church and Holcombe Chapel, a still easier stroll.

Walks or drives may be taken up the valley, at the back of the town, past the church and between rows of elm trees, to the summit of Great or Little Haldon. A specially fine view over the Teign estuary is obtained at a turn in the road about half-way up Little Haldon. About a mile back from the station, beside the road to Little Haldon, are the beautiful grounds of Luscombe, opened to the

public two days a week. They contain a private Chapel designed by Sir Gilbert Scott. A very pleasant walk (6 to 7 m.) may be enjoyed by continuing on this road to the summit of the Little Haldon Ridge, and dropping thence to Teignmouth. A shorter way to Teignmouth is taken by a lane to the left of the church, passing over Holcombe Down. The shortest, if not the most agreeable, is by the high road keeping a little back from the shore.

On the Starcross side, the sea wall gives a walk of over a mile to Langstone Point. But pleasanter is *the lane along the edge of the cliff in this direction, to be gained at more than one point by crossing the railway. A good round might thus be made by Starcross, Kenton and Mamhead.*

At the Teignmouth end, the cliffs are obstructed by private grounds; but one can take the direct Teignmouth road, then after a mile or more turn down at Lower Holcombe by 'Smugglers' Lane',

passing under the railway to regain the coast near the Parson and Clerk rocks, two prominent stacks of red sandstone which still hold their own, more or less, against the buffeting of the waves.

From this point it is about a mile and a half to Teignmouth by the sea wall, along which now runs the railway, after being boxed up in a succession of tantalising tunnels.

The King's Walk was built in 1901–2 as a protective wall for the railway line. The footbridge over the line and the railway tunnel disappearing into the cliff side can be seen in the background to the right of the boat cove.

2

The Countryside Around Dawlish

Its position at the edge of the English Channel, flanked by warm red sandstone cliffs, has made Dawlish an ideal holiday venue. The building of the railway confirmed this status as easy access was then made possible for the people of the Midlands and North who chose the South Devon coast as their favourite destination.

But though the sea and sand were its principal attractions, the countryside immediately inland from the town was as picturesque as any in the West Country. Flanked by the estuaries of the Exe and the Teign, the landscape is dotted with little settlements, often of thatched cottages and farmsteads reached through deep winding lanes. Around almost every corner there is some treat or other to meet the eye.

Down the steep valley runs Dawlish Water which rises high up on Haldon whose wooded hills form a backdrop to this most delightful of Devon scenes.

Dawlish Water, 1910. The ford now has a bridge over it.

HAPPY MEMORIES

Devonshire is beautiful, a dreaming country, of gentle rolling hills, steep valleys, high deep hedges full of wildlife and flowers. They shelter narrow secret lanes, opening at intervals to views of great beauty, with luscious fields, low thatched granite farms, and old lopsided cottages. Winding rivers within large shallow estuaries combine with ancient high mysterious moors, and such a varied coastline of 'rouge' sandstone and limestone cliffs. All this with historic ports, towns of different sizes and little villages, made such an impression on me, growing up in Devon, first Exeter, then Dawlish, that its soul is deep in my heart for ever, with so many happy memories.

Dawlish is such a peaceful place to grow up in. Miles of sand and sea, walks up to Haldon, to the clear air of the moors, with their spectacular views. A favourite walk of mine, the long walk either along the sea walls, or beaches from Dawlish to Dawlish Warren. To tramp across the pooled sands with their half buried groynes and the dunes, to the point opposite Exmouth. Going around the point to the mudflats and marshes was the lovely estuary where many varieties of birdlife could be spotted, and so many little boats and yachts, at anchor or busily going in and out, either up the river to Countess Wear, Exeter, or on out to the open sea.

A man and his dog stand under Luscombe Arch, better known locally as Aller Arch, 1908.

Children stand with a water pail at Brown's Brook Cottage, 1907.

Beech trees create a leafy arch above Barton Lane, 1908.

Two boys collect firewood at Newhay Bridge, 1907.

A reminder of rural times and farming methods in Victorian days. These thatched ricks stand at the Bartons in 1890, then belonging to farmer Bill Williams. They will stand until the spring when the corn will be threshed. A winter wood pile is seen on the left.

Workmen at the piggeries which stood behind the sawmill at Home Farm on the Luscombe Estate, 1880.

The Warren Copse with the Round House in the distance, 1900.

Gathering blackberries on Stockton Hill, 1908. This sunken lane is typical of many South Devon byways. Centuries of traffic have worn a deep path between high sandstone banks.

Oxon Lane, Dawlish Water, 1910. A simple footbridge suffices for pedestrians whilst, in days before motor traffic, the ford allows passage of cattle and farm wagons. Note that the road is unmetalled at this date.

A horseman poses in the sunken lane on Stockton Hill, 1908.

3
Luscombe Castle and Park

The Luscombe Estate was purchased by Charles Hoare at the end of the seventeenth century. He employed John Nash to design the castle and Humphrey Repton created the parkland. The building took four years to complete.

According to a guidebook of the time 'every comfort which can be commanded by wealth and art has been secured. An excellent organ, by England, stands in the staircase hall, where a gothic stained window imparts a rich ecclesiastical effect.'

Sixty years later St Albans Chapel was built on the south side of the house to commemorate the original Charles Hoare and intended for the use of the family, servants and estate workers. Gilbert Scott used three different types of stone in its construction.

At about this time public access was allowed to the estate although by 1900 the footpaths were closed to local people. However, many public occasions and events were held in the parkland in front of the castle.

Luscombe Castle, c.1900. On the left is St Albans Chapel opened in 1862.

Weech from the Newhay. Stonelands at Weech Hill was built in 1820 as a dower house to Luscombe, but the whole scene is very different today as bungalows and houses occupy much of this area.

A summer fête at Luscombe in 1924.

This aircraft, a DeHavilland DH9C, was set down in the 'twenty-acre field' at Luscombe in 1923 just behind the area now occupied by the South Downs Road estate. The pilot was Hubert Broad, chief test pilot at DeHavilland's and he had flown down to Dawlish in order to pick up Alan Butler, Chairman of DeHavilland's, and his friend Sir Peter Hoare and take them back to London.

4
The Beaches and Seafront

Certainly since it grew to be one of Devon's principal seaside resorts towards the end of the nineteenth century, the focus of attention on Dawlish, for summer visitors at least, has rested on its beaches and the seafront. These sandy stretches, ribbed with wooden groynes to prevent erosion, run for almost a mile and a half between Langstone Rock at its northern end and Old Maid Rock in the south, with Coryton Cove hidden a little way beyond.

The railway line passes along the coast at this point between the town and the sea and gives an unusual feeling of separation between the two. However, passing trains provide a unique attraction to those who are enjoying the sands. A guidebook for 1859 describes the town as follows:

The aspect of Dawlish is bright and cheering. The railway runs across the mouth of the valley. Opinions differ as to its affect upon the appearance of the place; but the taste of Mr Brunel has been shown in a small granite viaduct in a plain Egyptian style, which carries the rail across the brook, and affords a free communication with the shore. The railway company have also formed a handsome esplanade along the side of the line.

The effect of the line has been to keep buildings back from the beaches, thus retaining the character of the old town whilst preventing the blight of modern buildings which have sprung up along the seafront of so many other resorts.

In this photograph, taken c.1913, it is interesting to note the required beach-wear of the day. Only the child seems comfortably attired for the sun and the sand. The bathing machines in the background were pulled in and out of the waves, allowing women to enter the water with their modesty intact!

Left: *The original caption to this superb photograph c.1905 reads: 'Mr and Mrs Coombs - Mary Anne and "The Admiral", Henry Coombs, on the main beach.' The potential of the bathing machines for carrying advertisements has been fully realised.*

Below: *The sea is not always so benign and here, c.1920, a late summer storm crashes waves over the sea wall.*

A LUCKY ESCAPE

A nasty incident happened one summer, which could have easily turned into a tragedy. We had all been swimming in a fairly rough sea, by the breakwater on the little beach by the old Coastguard hut, the tide had turned to go out, when my mother's friend, Marie Bailey, was caught by the undertow, and was swept out very quickly far off shore. All we could see was the little white dot of her bathing cap and a limp hand waving for help. Her husband bravely tried to swim out to rescue her, he tried again and again but the waves dashed him back against the breakwater and the barnacles cut his legs badly and he had to be rescued. The coastguards were alerted and the lifeboat and a fishing boat came out from Dawlish, we were all very frightened as we thought there was no hope for her. But the boat caught up with her just in time, as she was going down in the water. What an ordeal, but she soon recovered, but we did not attempt to bathe in such rough seas again.

Coryton Cove c.1917. The little changing tents stand in front of more permanent wooden huts ranged along the foot of the cliff. In the background is the breakwater which originally was not joined to the cliff. The GWR in the 1920s filled in the last portion and constructed a light railway to carry materials along the breakwater.

THE BOOK OF DAWLISH

Left: *The King's Walk, c.1910. A young man sits on the sea wall reading the morning paper, while couples stroll the esplanade taking in the sea air. Bathing costumes and towels are pegged out to dry in readiness for those who fancy a dip in the afternoon.*

Below: *A fine view of Coryton Cove, c.1910. At this time the cove was a men-only bathing beach – for modesty's sake – although both men's and boys' bathing costumes of the day covered all but the extremities.*

A LUCKY ESCAPE

I remember hiring a little rowing boat sometimes from the fisherman's cove to row my little brother, Geoff, about in the bay. You could see porpoises then, swiftly going through the water, diving and leaping. One day I had to ship my oars in the boat as we were surrounded by inquisitive porpoises, fins above the water and diving under the boat, a lovely sight, then in a flash they were off and gone. A good job I had not seen the horror film 'Jaws' then, or the fins and shapes around us may have taken on a more sinister form!

An early photograph, c.1868, showing the coastguard's cottage. In the background is Seaview House, demolished c.1887.

This panoramic view of the seafront (c.1902) from the station shows the distinctive position of the town in relation to the beach. The 'Egyptian' railway viaduct was built by the cele-brated engineer Isambard Kingdom Brunel, who also designed and constructed the railway.

A wonderful postcard view of Coryton Cove and beyond to the famous landmarks of the Parson and Clerk rock formation.

5
Storms and Floods

Being close to the sea brings its perils as well as its pleasures and, although Dawlish has escaped the fate of some South Devon villages that have been lost entirely to the waves, it has had its share of alarms. The incessant rains of the winter of 2000–2001 brought floods, and before that, in 1960, severe flooding occurred when heavy rainfall combined with high tides saw parts of the town under water. On that occasion waves sweeping under the viaduct prevented the brook water draining into the sea with the result that York Gardens and nearby streets were under water.

Snowfalls are rare in South Devon, and heavy falls rarer still, but the photographs in this section provide ample evidence of storms, gales and blizzards of the past.

WINTER STORMS

I recall some fierce winter storms, delicious, when you are inside, in the warmth and safety of your house, to watch the spray from a rough sea thunder and hiss over the sea wall, railway lines and path and swish against our windows. But there was often a lot of damage as the long waves picked up stones, shingle, shells and seaweed in their green hands, and hurled it with great force, leaving it strewn everywhere on the sea walls, lines, our paths and gardens. Often too, breaking great holes in the sea walls, like cannons in a war, flooding the lines and causing many delays until the railway men could repair the defences and make the tracks safe again. I remember several times, the long wooden platform at Dawlish Station being smashed in places, delaying trains for days. So you took the rough with the smooth, the unpredictable sea, a raging tiger at times, at other times, a gentle smiling pussycat.

Storm damage to the railway line and sea wall, c.1870.

Beach huts on stilts in the 1920s and '30s. These were allowed on the beach during the summer months and were always vulnerable to end-of-season storms.

Waves broke down the sea wall at Black Bridge in 1962 and the upline was called into use for downline trains.

Further damage caused by the storm of 1962; here rails are buckled and ballast washed away.

Run-off from the rains on the hills behind the town could be catastrophic. Here, on 19 October 1875, a bridge in the Lawn is wrecked by the swollen brook.

Below: *More damage caused by the flood.*

Dawlish sea wall, built to protect the railway line, had been a controversial subject in the town for many years. The wall and the track have often been damaged by storms, sometimes causing long delays in train services. In November 1908 several hundred feet of wall was washed away.

A truly remarkable photograph of man's ingenuity battling against nature's elements, 1960.

Also in the storms of 1960, small boats are pulled up out of reach of the waves.

Waves batter the Coastguard station in a winter storm, 1907.

Heavy falls of snow are infrequent in South Devon and are mainly confined to the uplands of Haldon and nearby Dartmoor. The winter of 1962 was an exception, for Dawlish and most of Great Britain was caught in the grip of one of the most severe winters on record. The photographs on this page give some idea of the severity of that arctic winter.

Deep snow and bitter temperatures for weeks on end characterised the winter of 1962. Road and rail traffic was paralysed, schools closed and homes were without water, sometimes for weeks.

6
Fishing and Fishermen

With other ports being blessed with more secure harbours, fishing was never an important part of the economic life of Dawlish. However, many small boats were engaged in the fishing trade, often supplying local needs. Early photographs show small boats drawn up on the shore, especially in the sheltered boat cove. In those days herrings and pilchards were plentiful and men would go out with nets to encircle the shoals, bringing their silver horde back on to the beach to be sold.

As fish stocks dwindled and the fishing industry also fell into decline around the end of the nineteenth century so fishermen found lucrative alternative employment in taking summer visitors on boat trips around the bay.

These days fishing is largely done for fun, or for supplying domestic needs. With fish stocks dangerously low and some species having almost vanished fishing is very localised and most boating is now recreational.

This photograph indicates the relative importance of fishing in Dawlish up to the end of the nineteenth century. Fishing boats were sail powered and seldom travelled far from shore for their catch. However, the pride of the men engaged in fishing is evident from this photograph taken in 1886. They are celebrating the opening of the new fishermen's and boatmen's shelter.

THE OLD FISHERMEN

Opposite our house there was a little bridge over which my Mother would take my brother and myself to the fishermen's cove with a long breakwater wall, from which you could fish. Some fishing boats and pleasure boats lay bobbing gently in the water, others were drawn up on the sand and shingle. We spent hours watching the mostly old fishermen, in their high boots and old darned jerseys and even older caps, smoking their pipes and woodbines and mending the odd net or remaking a broken lobster pot.

Huge shoals of herring frequented the shallow seas around the coast and were much prized by fishermen. Once they had been salted down they would last for many months and provided a rich source of food during winter months.

A superb photograph of the Boat Cove taken on a warm summer's day. The little fishing fleet is drawn up on the shingle while, to the right of the picture, boats are undergoing repair and maintenance. In the centre is the second incarnation of the fishermen's shelter, this being opened in 1907. To ensure good order a notice proclaimed 'No Intoxicants, No Gambling.'

Herring being packed into hogsheads to be taken to market, quite possibly by train, c.1910.

SILVER HARVEST

Sometimes, at certain times of the year, the tide would bring in masses of tiny fish. We and others, and the fishermen, would wait at the shoreline with nets and buckets. The sea would ripple with the silvery fire of many leaping, threshing tiny fish and shoals of glistening little sprats would come boiling on to the shoreline. Whirlpools and eddies further out meant that bigger fish, mackerel, etc. were after them in an orgy of feeding. You could literally wade in the shallow water and scoop up buckets of them to carry them home all frisky and squirming, poor things, but there was nothing tastier than fried sprats for supper.

Below: *Two sharks caught at Dawlish in 1907. The fisherman third from right is Ernie Cotton, one of the last fulltime fishermen in Dawlish.*

Boatmen posing proudly with their catch of sprats, c.1900. Note the traditional sweaters and caps.

Another good haul lies in a fishing boat waiting to be sorted and sold. By 1910, when this photograph was taken, fishing in Dawlish was already in decline. Large motor trawlers were taking the place of small sailing craft and supplying the larger urban market with cheap, plentiful fish, usually transported by train.

The final version of the fishermen's shelter, opened in 1937. It is interesting to compare this photograph with the two earlier views of this location. By the late 1930s seaside resorts such as Dawlish were enjoying something of a heyday. Cheap railway travel brought visitors in their thousands to South Devon, usually to stay in Bed & Breakfast accommodation, often hosted by seaside landladies. Money brought into the town meant local authorities could afford to pave the promenade and generally provide better public amenities. The transition from fishing to tourism is apparent in this photograph which shows holidaymakers relaxing on benches under the verandah of the shelter, while in the foreground a sign advertises the White Rose *motor vessel for hire, with mackerel fishing around the bay. In his photo albums, Bernard Chapman records the names of some of the last Dawlish fishermen as H. Bully (later a fish dealer); T. Casely; J. and F. Cross (who were also painters); T.J. Combstock; G. Monk; J. Briscoe; T. Ash; F. Combstock (who was drowned when his boat capsized in the bay during a regatta race); B. Crewys (also a boatbuilder); F. Dart (later a council employee); J. Rackley (great-grandfather); T. Rackley (grandfather); Dick Rackley (son); R. Rackley (grandson); C. and E. Cotton; W. Cotton (father of A. Cotton and Wm Cotton; Bob King; T. Spicer; W. Horsfield (the last three being Victorian Naval Pensioners); J. 'Sparks' Gilpin; J. Voysey (grandfather); G. Voysey (father); W. Voysey (son); H. Reed (father); E. Reed (son); T. Frost.*

7

The Railway

The coming of the railway had a profound effect on Dawlish. Before the advent of rail travel the small community would have been very much cut off from the rest of the country, with narrow lanes allowing passage into the hinterland for farm wagons and packhorses. Not that many would travel far – they had no need. Perhaps an occasional trip to Exeter would be taken, probably on foot, or possibly by boat.

By 1844 the Bristol and Exeter Railway (later the Great Western Railway) had reached Exeter and the pre-eminent engineer of his day, Isambard Kingdom Brunel, began to plan the next stage of the route via the west bank of the River Exe to Dawlish Warren, then on to Dawlish, Teignmouth and routes west.

The difficulties of building a permanent way along this section tested Brunel's skill to the limit and involved building the line behind a massive sea wall and taking the track though various tunnels dug through the cliffs. Six tunnels alone were necessary to carry the line between Dawlish and Teignmouth. To add to the problems he decided to install an atmospheric railway along the route from Exeter to Plymouth, a novel system and largely untried.

His innovative design involved the use of a hollow rail in which a piston, fixed to the train, was pulled along by the force of a vacuum created by pumping air out of the hollow rail. Leather flaps which closed along the top of the rail maintained pressure inside after the train (and the piston) had passed by. Huge pumping stations were built at three-mile intervals in order to draw the air out of the rail. One stood in the Dawlish goods yard, another at Starcross.

The first train ran from Exeter to Turf and back in February 1847, and by September of that year trains were carrying passengers as far as Teignmouth. However, the railway was beset with problems. Seawater affected the leather seals and air leaked into the system overburdening the pumps. The piston itself was damaged and its own seals destroyed. Though in theory the

Brunel's atmospheric railway line at Dawlish with the pumping house alongside, c.1847.

atmospheric railway had advantages over steam, in truth it was a disaster and, within a year, Brunel was forced to revert to more conventional methods of propulsion.

At that time there were four stations in the area, two at Dawlish and two at the Warren. The original Dawlish station was an open wooden shed and it was not until this burnt down in 1873 that it was replaced by buildings of stone. This was opened in 1875.

Dawlish Warren Halt was opened in 1905 in order to cater for the day trippers who would flock from Exeter to the coast on hot summer days. The Halt was some distance from the location of the present station and was sited below the footbridge crossing the rails below Mount Pleasant. A second station, called Dawlish Warren, was opened in

1912 a quarter of a mile from the Halt. This station was also burnt down, in 1924, but was later rebuilt.

The original broad gauge line was single line track, converted to double track into Dawlish by 1847. On 21 and 22 May 1892 the broad-gauge track was converted to standard gauge, although a third rail had been added to parts of the track in advance of this date in order to speed up the conversion.

Track through the Dawlish–Teignmouth tunnels remained single gauge until widening took place from 1902 to 1905.

The importance of the railway to Dawlish and its development is illustrated through the many photographs included here.

In 1853 the railway bridge at Holcombe was destroyed in a storm.

A cliff fall blocks the line at Parson's tunnel. The waiting locomotive is a Comet-class saddle tank built in 1851–2. These pictures illustrate just some of the difficulties faced by those building the line. Unstable cliffs, rough seas, the effects of salt air on track and trains, all added to the cost of building and maintaining the line.

The picture on the left contains a host of detail regarding Dawlish c.1870. Bathing machines are scattered across the beach and beyond them a train stands at (the first) Dawlish station, opened in 1846. Brunel's viaduct, allowing access to the beach from the town, is visible, as are the pillars supporting the station platform which juts out over the sea wall. Beyond them is the atmospheric pumping station with its Italianate campanile. The dark patches on the beach are fishing nets laid out to dry – an indication of the importance of the fishing industry at that time.

Below: The first Dawlish station building, opened in 1846 and destroyed by fire in 1873. The Royal Hotel and the annexe to the Grand, familiar landmarks to later generations, had not been built at this time. A carriage sits to the right and a donkey beyond. These would be for hire to take passengers and goods to and from the station.

Railway staff pose proudly for their photograph at the first Dawlish station, c.1870. Note the paper boy on the right, the carrier's cart on the left, and the porters with their hand trucks waiting for the arrival of the next train.

The first Dawlish Warren station, opened in 1905 and closed in 1912. Compare this with the view of the second station (below), pictured in 1914 two years after its opening. On that occasion the Union Flag was hoisted and detonators placed on the line in celebration.

The Teignmouth tunnel and cutting as depicted in an engraving dated before 1884.

Compare this picture with that above. Taken in 1957 it shows the same stretch of line running into Teignmouth but with the cutting replacing Brunel's tunnel and a bridge carrying the road over the line.

The last broad-gauge train from Paddington to Penzance between Holcombe and Teignmouth, 20 May 1892. Note the track where every second transom has been cut to save time during the conversion from broad to narrow gauge.

In 1920 Parson's tunnel was lengthened by 129 yards in order to bypass unstable cliffs, falls from which often blocked the line. During the work, two Dawlish men, T. Curry and C. Moyse, were hit by a passing train and killed.

The west entrance of Coryton tunnel, in 1964, showing the original arch built for broad gauge trains and the portion widened on the right side only to cater for the doubled track.

The single-line, broad-gauge track which existed between 1846 and 1892.

A similar view, c.1892, to that above, but showing the third line added in preparation for the change from broad to narrow gauge.

Below: *The scene on the afternoon of 21 May 1892 showing the change-over of gauge in progress.*

While we were growing up in the Mendip Hills, Somerset, little did my mother realise that one day in the future, she would live with her young family right beside the most beautiful stretch of railway line in Devon. Each day we watched the steam trains huffing and puffing around the curved track beside the sandy beaches edging the glittering blue green expanses of sea. Her family back in Somerset had listened with wonder to one old uncle's story, of a recently spent holiday in Dawlish and of the railway. They said 'You are pulling our legs, trains running beside the sea, for miles and miles'. But of course it was true, although to my mother and her family, all farmers, in 1906, holidays were a very rare event in their lives, and the description of Dawlish was met with disbelief.

Top: *A photograph taken c.1903 showing the 'Kennet' locomotive, one of the famous Dean singles, coming into the station. Note the whelk stall on the beach.*

Centre: *Some time after 1905 showing the double track.*

Left: *A star class locomotive pulls into Dawlish GWR station, 1908.*

Scenes from a railway accident which occurred on 22 September 1921 when the north-bound express hit a goods train that was being transferred from the up to the down line.

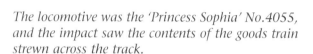

The locomotive was the 'Princess Sophia' No.4055, and the impact saw the contents of the goods train strewn across the track.

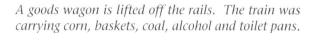

A goods wagon is lifted off the rails. The train was carrying corn, baskets, coal, alcohol and toilet pans.

RAILWAY MEMORIES

We arrived in Dawlish in an old red sports car (a vintage collectable now), driving down the winding hill, to the lawns and stream, and stopped at last right beside the first big tunnel which leads on through other tunnels to Teignmouth. Towering above the tunnel was a large red cliff, Lea Mount, with paths winding around and leading to the summit, and the main road out of Dawlish to Teignmouth. Facing the line were a few large terraced houses, and to our delight we had rented a first floor flat, albeit only temporarily, in the second but one house nearest the tunnel. It seemed very strange at first living right beside the railway lines, getting used to the noise of the trains. They always gave a long, loud whistle and hoot before they entered the tunnel, to warn any gangers working on the track inside, then the train would disappear in clouds of steam, like a genie going back into his bottle. But we soon became acclimatised and loved to watch the trains and hear them.

Above: *Dawlish station, c.1922.*

Below: *GWR locomotive No.100, 'Dean' with the 6.15am Bristol to Newton Abbot postal train, 1902.*

RAILWAY MEMORIES

We got to know quite a few of the train drivers, so cheerful and friendly, with their red and sometimes sooty faces. The drivers, with caps jammed on the back of their heads, usually a pipe clenched in their teeth, leant with one arm on the cab window, and waved and shouted to us, acknowledging our waves and shouts, the stoker waved too, if he had time from shovelling the coal, and the drivers always pulled the whistle, to our glee. Our little terrier dog, Tony, was remarkable, and his exploits for racing the trains to the station were well known, and the *Dawlish Gazette* even printed his story once.

Three views of Dawlish in the golden age of steam. This view is c.1950, taken from the Royal Hotel looking across to the seafront, with the Blenheim Hotel opposite. Note the number of cars lined up – precursors to the plague of cars today.

Dawlish station in the late 1950s, with the Grand Hotel on the left. Note the Belisha beacon in the centre of the photograph, warning motorists of crossing pedestrians.

RAILWAY MEMORIES

Visitors have come to Dawlish for many years, for its lovely setting, and it still has a rather Victorian air about it. The railway station, like a toy station, with its long wooden platforms with the Porter crying 'Dawleesh' as the train comes in, sea walls beside the lines, the long stretches of beaches with their protective groynes trying to curb the sea's power, the gulls crying and wheeling overhead, the colours of the blue-grey sea, the red cliffs, the pretty brook running all through the town, it has always enchanted and still does.

A wonderful view of the line sweeping along the coast, a view familiar to millions who have travelled this route by train.

8
Marine Parade

Though traditional Devon houses from the pre-holiday resort of Dawlish survive here and there throughout the town, little of the early fishing settlement exists. In common with other seaside towns, old cottages, boat huts and fish stores were swept aside in the rush to build elegant homes and hotels immediately overlooking the sea. Dating from the early Victorian period through to the early 1920s, many of these substantial buildings have themselves undergone demolition or conversion into flats. Of the big hotels, among them The Grand, The Royal and The Blenheim, few remain.

These views are a reminder of this age of elegance, when gentlemen and ladies would promenade in the evenings, taking in the sea air, before retiring for the night.

Marine Parade, c.1868. The tower of Brunel's atmospheric railway pumping house is visible at the far right, and at this date the track is still the old broad gauge.

Marine Parade, c.1880. The Bathing Pavilion, built in 1879, is visible in this photograph, in the centre of the Parade. Note also the iron footbridge over the railway which was removed and replaced by a concrete bridge in 1965.

Below: 1873, and the station is seen here under construction. On the beach, bathing machines vie for space with drying fishing nets. There used to be a small tunnel for pedestrian access on part of Lea Mount and its entrance can just be glimpsed on the left of this photo.

The Bathing Pavilion

These two photographs, taken thirty years apart, show some interesting changes in that time, although the essential scene remains much the same. The top photograph was taken c.1911, the lower one in 1948.

9
Around the Town

In this section of the book we look at some of the streets, shops and houses of Dawlish. The surprising thing revealed through looking at the photographs is perhaps not how much change has been effected over the last hundred years or so, but how little. Dawlish is indeed fortunate that so much of the early layout of the town remains visible and how many of its elegant buildings, small cottages, shops and houses are still intact.

Among the greatest changes perhaps have been those made to accommodate the motor car. Today everywhere the streets are full of parked cars. Car parks are overburdened, especially in summer, and signposts, yellow lines and traffic lights litter the scene. Thankfully, although highly visible, these are largely temporary impositions on the townscape. Hopefully in the future something of its earlier calm and elegance may be restored.

Two views of Old Town Street. The view above, taken in 1870, is recognisable even today, although the cottage on the hill has been demolished and some of the houses in the street are gone. More changes are evident in the photograph on the left with none of the cottages in the foreground now surviving.

How tranquil life appears in these three photographs of Old Town Street taken in 1908. Such was the novelty of photography that people came out into the street to pose for the photographer. In the top photograph are the premises of W.R. Williams, coal and coke merchant, and next door Way's lamp and oil shop of Way. The horse and cart belongs to the chimney sweep. Schoolboys pose on the pavement to the left.

In the middle photograph it is the turn of the women and girls to have their photographs taken, the girls in their starched pinafores, and a young shop assistant stands in his apron on the left.

The lower picture is taken further down Old Town Street. The general store on the left, Ferris's, has a pair of rabbits hanging over the door. Opposite is the Red Lion Inn where stands the village postman in his distinctive uniform.

Two views of Queen Street in 1908. The gardens in the upper picture disappeared when the street was widened in the 1960s. Here are seen the shops of Cox and Moore, and Davey's the butcher's premises.

Left: *The corner of Park Street and Regent Street, c.1910. A notice in the West End Post Office advertises low-cost fares to Canada.*

Below: *Cows being driven down Church Street in 1946. All the old cottages were pulled down to make way for old people's bungalows in 1950.*

Above and right: *Church cottages as seen in 1907. These buildings were demolished following a fire in 1913 and the site is now occupied by the war memorial.*

Wysteria-covered thatched cottages on Badlake Hill, 1906. Note that all the roads were unmetalled in those days and, in the summer, water carts toured the town in order to damp down the dust.

Refined Edwardian elegance is evident in this photograph of Barton Villas in 1906.

Looking down the Strand in 1908. Messrs Cridge & Sons were then the under-takers.

Looking up the Strand c.1890. On the right is the London (formerly South-wood's) Hotel which later became the site of Woolworth's. In the centre is Shapter's store, then gas fitters and ironmongers.

A similar view twenty years later, looking up the Strand in 1908. Shapter's store now advertises Shell motor spirit. On the left milk churns stand in a horse-drawn cart outside the dairy.

DAWLISH SHOPS

Dawlish had some fine old houses and quaint shops. If the seas were rough and breaking over the sea walls we walked to town by the roads. The stream or brook was so pretty through the centre with lawns and flower beds, an infinite variety of colourful ducks and the famous pairs of black swans, which Dawlish has always been known to have, as long as I can remember. Each side of the brook and lawns were genteel Victorian and Edwardian private houses, a few boarding houses and hotels and a variety of shops. There were love-ly old-fashioned grocery shops with long wooden counters, tins and bottles stacked on shelves, cardboard advertising posters stood on the counters with bacon slicers and cheese cutters, and bins and tubs full of food ready to be weighed out on brass scales standing on the floor. The shopkeepers and assistants wore long pinafores, sometimes white, often striped, with strings tying them in the front. Shirtsleeves rolled up with false white sleeves pulled over these to keep their clothes clean, secured with armbands. They all wore dark bow ties and were all so very courteous and helpful and knew their customers' names. Further along there were ornate-fronted dress and haberdashery shops with large linen blinds ready to be pulled up and down at the first ray of sunshine on the large glass win-dows. Only a few discreet items were displayed: dresses, some hats with gloves to match, a scarf, or one coat or a fur stole. Rarely any undies, you had to go inside to see those, and the pink boned-and-laced corsets of the day, dreadful contraptions those and liberty bodices, we had to wear in winter. At one side of the dress shops was a large double-fronted hairdressers, the other a good bakers and teashop – Hunts' Bakery. In the bakery was a long glass-fronted counter where you were served bread and cakes. In the other half of the shop glass-topped tables were arranged with four bamboo chairs to each table for customers to partake of morning tea (no coffee served then), with cakes or scones and afternoon teas. The family became friends of ours, Barbara, the daughter, was in my school, and Michael, the brother, was a very good friend of my brother Colin and myself for many years. These so pleasant shops and premises have now become Amusement Arcades, Estate Agents, etc. and retain little of their former charm. The hairdressers lived in a flat above their working premises, where, later on in hot little cubicles, my mother and I braved the five-hour perms, permanent waves indeed! You sat strung up in the hot curlers to a terrifying machine, the 'Eugine perm-waving Machine', an ordeal all through. Halftime you were brought a reviv-ing pot of tea and a plate of biscuits, which you certainly needed, as by then your face was scarlet and you were quite dehydrated. Eventually you emerged with a massive frizz of tight, tight curls and waves and a horrid smell of singed hair. It is a wonder we had any hair left at all, but unless a perm lasted a good 7–8 months, it was not considered a good perm, or your money's worth.

The corner shop in Beach Lane, c.1890. Compare this with the view on page 9. The window advertises 'Pure Ice Cream', while the signs beyond are for the Railway Inn and the Exeter Inn, just two of the fourteen public houses that could be found in Dawlish at the end of the nineteenth century. Others were: the London Hotel, the Royal Albert Hotel, the York Hotel, the Prince of Wales Inn, the Teignmouth Inn, the White Hart, the South Devon Inn, the Red Lion, the Swan, the Manor Inn, the Brunswick Arms, the Royal Hotel, the Carpenters' Arms and the New Inn. More recently there have been the Devon Arms, the Lansdowne Hotel, the Gresham Arms (latterly the Greasy Pig), and the Prince Albert Inn (latterly the Hole in the Wall).

The Teignmouth Inn on Teignmouth Hill, c.1915.

Piermont Place, c.1900. Alongside Matthews Piermont Stores, are Griffins the tobacconist and Averys general store.

Piermont Place, c.1910. This row was later occupied by the Daw Vale Creamery and Florist, Sheppard's Amusements and the Fountain Café.

Piermont Place, c.1938. By this time W.H. Smith & Son were established here (the newspaper stand proclaims 'Italian Offensive in Ogaden'), next to the hair salon and the Daw Vale Dairy. Further down the street is Brunt's Café.

An early view of Piermont Place c.1880 with Hatcher's Royal Hotel. Note the donkeys at the bottom right-hand corner of the photograph. Donkey rides were a popular beach attraction for many years.

The Royal Hotel in 1908 with the station beyond and the Grand Hotel to the left of the footbridge. On the right is the cabman's shelter (later moved to the lower end of the Lawn). Note the complete absence of motorised traffic.

A similar view to above but taken in 1935. The Royal Hotel now flaunts a sign for the Automobile Association and the Royal Automobile Club although horse-drawn cabs are still very much in use.

Right and below: *Two very early photographs of Barton Terrace (looking east and west respectively), taken c.1865. At the time these photographs were taken the present-day route from Barton Hill to the church was blocked by a house opposite the Knowle.*

Below: *Barton Crescent, 1908. Note the little girl playing with a hoop.*

High Street 1908. A carrier's handcart is parked outside Cornelius's store.

Hatcher Street in 1908. The photographer clearly caught the attention of many of the street's inhabitants.

Iddesleigh Terrace in 1927. The Exeter Road Garage can be seen at the end of the street.

Brook Street in 1908. The Manor Inn can be seen at the top of the street and Stone's stores on the left. Almost every street at this time had its corner shop.

Another view of Brook Street in 1908. The Manor Inn can be seen on the right.

Alexandra Place in 1908.

Top left: *Lane's Tea Cottage, Badlake Hill, c.1927.*

Above: *Tudor Cottages, High Street, c.1910. These are much the same today.*

Left: *Town Tree Hill in 1936. Note the cobbled pavements.*

King Street, 1920.

Brookdale, c.1860. This handsome cottage once stood where Brookdale Terrace was later built. The grass in the foreground was latterly incorporated into a putting green.

Two views of Marine Parade and Teignmouth Hill dating from around 1860. The shop in the centre occupies a site later filled by the Blenheim Hotel. The Teignmouth Inn is seen on the right standing above the thatched cottage which was later replaced by the National Provincial Bank.

Higher up Teignmouth Hill, c.1890. The two-storey building with the balcony is Lisburne House, later becoming the Lisburne Hotel.

Tudor Cottage, High Street, c.1922. Standing outside with the policeman are Frank Bolt and Sam Murch the 'Okey Pokey Man' who sold ice cream.

West Cliff, Teignmouth Hill, c.1910.

The Strand, c.1920. On the left is W.P. Crapp's dairy and greengrocer's premises.

Lawn Terrace, c.1915.

Lanherne Corner in 1965 before demolition of the Lodge to accommodate road widening.

Albert Street decorated for the Coronation celebrations in 1937.

10
Shops and Businesses

Commerce is still at the heart of all communities and for Dawlish this has long meant businesses that are associated with the tourism industry, from campsites and hotels to taxis and deck chairs.

The explosion of summer visitors in seaside towns created a rapid growth in shops and businesses directly catering for their holiday needs. People came to Dawlish to enjoy themselves and, along with the suppliers of essentials, shops sprang up which were devoted entirely to the provision of souvenirs. These were shops selling beachwear, buckets and spades, rock (with 'Dawlish' written all the way through it), small pottery gifts emblazoned with the town crest, postcard views and, of course, clotted cream to be sent by post.

Almost all these shops were privately owned by local families. The photographs in this section were taken in the days before small supermarket chains drove out the individual shopkeepers and made once uniquely distinctive towns indistinguishable one from another.

I.W. Hole's grocery store in Park Road, c.1920. Later to become Brimble's shoe shop.

The London Restaurant, the Strand, c.1920. It was owned by E. Cridge and later the premises became part of Woolworth's.

Cornelius & Son, fruiterers, c.1920. The shop stood at the foot of Teignmouth Hill and was demolished to make way for a bank.

Eardley & Hobden's wine and grocery store, Piermont Place, c.1960. At that time it was owned by G.S. Merrill and later became a Victoria Wine shop.

In 1956 a new Woolworth's store was constructed next to the Midland Bank.

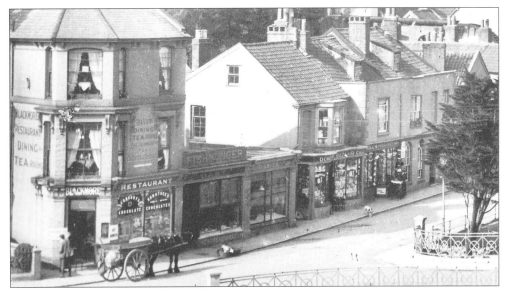

The seafront end of Brunswick Place, c.1912, with Blackmore's Restaurant (which later became H & B Capener's gift shop), and Mrs Butler's York Café.

Humphries' Lansdowne Hotel, Park Road, c.1915.

This is Harris's Commercial Temperance Hotel as seen c.1910. It later became part of Richmond Garages.

The Red Lion Inn, Old Town Street, c.1925. Its thatched roof was replaced in 1932.

Bridge House, 1912, was built as a private residence but was taken over by the Great Western Railway company as a convalescent home in July 1918.

The London Hotel, c.1900.

The London Hotel, c.1920, following extensive restoration. It was later replaced by Woolworth's and the Midland Bank buildings. It was later purchased by the council, in September 1910, so that the main road into Dawlish might be widened. At this time the road at the foot of Strand Hill and Iddesleigh Terrace was only 12 feet. It was widened to 28 feet.

Brook House, Old Town Street, c.1900. Originally a private house, it later became an old people's home.

Williams & Son coalyards in Old Town Street, c.1880.

Hopkins & Sons garage, Piermont Place, c.1915. This later became Greenslade's coach station.

Cox, the drapers, at Queen Street, c.1920. This later became the premises of Mrs Allen, also a draper. Note the huge bolts of cloth in the window, and also the gas lamp over the shop door.

A carrier's cart waits outside Yellands Stores in Piermont Place, c.1884.

Left: *The Haldon Tea House, c.1936. This stood where the lane from Bishopsteignton and Haldon golf course joins the Teignmouth–Exeter road. At a later date it became a private bungalow.*

Below: *The Worlds Stores and staff outside the premises in the Strand, c.1964. This later became Key Markets.*

S.W. Chapman, Piermont Place, c.1935. The shop sold photographic equipment and film, along with postcards and fancy goods.

H.S. Loram, tailor, at 4 Prospect Place, c.1910. This building later became the premises for Dawlish Conservative Club.

DAWLISH SHOPS

On the left-hand side of the brook and lawns were a few shops, an old mill with its huge still-working waterwheel, which included a dairy and bakers, Gays. You could get the most delicious clotted cream served on home-made ice cream. One shop, an old-fashioned gentlemen's outfitters called Soundys, was where my brother Colin worked as an apprentice before going to war in the RAF. A few tiny bookshops and some old private houses comprised the rest of the street, apart from a lovely old church, St Marks. Going up the main High Street opposite there were some pretty quaint shops, a few private houses with elegant low windows and little formal front gardens. The chemists shop used to have large brilliantly-coloured glass bottles on shelves in the windows catching and reflecting the light and sunshine on bright days. A paper shop and lending library, long, low, rather dim premises, where for a few pennies each week, you could take two or three books out for a month which my mother often did. Next door, a little confectionery shop, with rows of bottled sweets and beautifully decorated boxes of chocolate, sometimes we managed to buy a few sweets on our way up to the Scala cinema. Halfway up was a large elegant double-fronted ladies' dress establishment with a men's tailoring shop next door. The tailoring shop usually displayed a few bolts of material lengths for suits with prices written in beautifully embellished writing on cards beside them. The last shop then was a butcher's shop which mother often used. Any orders, large or small, could always be delivered to your home the same day, either by lads on big bicycles or tricycles with a big basket on the front, and sometimes by horse and cart.

11

The Post Office

With the introduction of the Royal Mail by Rowland Hill and the advent of the Penny Black stamp the modern-day postal service was born. In recent times rapid means of sending messages by phone, fax and email has superseded some of the functions previously carried out by post, yet the mail continues to be a vital part of our lives and the postman an essential member of the community.

A letter-receiving office was opened in Dawlish in 1799 and in 1828 the first Post Office was opened in Mill Row (now Brunswick Place), with John Lowe as postmaster. Various offices followed at Piermont Place in 1838, Strand Hill in 1879, West End in 1892, the Strand in 1904, with a new office in Brunswick Place in 1959.

With the coming of the railway postal services rapidly improved with postal deliveries in the town sometimes three times each day. It was possible to post a letter in London in the morning and receive it in Dawlish in the afternoon. A device designed to catch mail bags suspended from a moving train was set up at Dawlish in the 1890s.

In 1893 the first telephone exchange was opened, with three subscribers. A public call office was established as the post office in 1913, and an automatic exchange installed in 1941.

The following pictures provide a clear reminder of the important role played by the postal service in Dawlish over the years.

A group of postmen outside the post office in the Strand, c.1906. Names include Kerswell, Willmet, Stokes, Luscombe, Frost and Moggridge. Up to 1904 Dawlish post offices had always been in premises provided by the postmaster or postmistress but after that time the GPO took over the lease of the premises in the Strand where the office remained for the next fifty years save for a brief period following a fire in 1908.

Above: *A remarkable picture of a mail bag being caught in a special net as the express speeds through Dawlish. This device allowed mails to be picked up and delivered without the train having to stop.*

Left: *Postman Fred Mallett and one of the first mail vans to be used in the Dawlish area. The photograph was taken in 1941 and shows the van with blackout devices on its head-lights and white linings on its wings, part of the wartime regulations.*

Right: *Local postmen being presented with certificates for safe driving by Jack Lamacraft. The photograph was taken in 1957 at the Strand.*

A temporary sorting office at Shaftesbury Hall, set up to cope with Christmas mail in 1953.

A group of post-men and the postmaster T.S. Wallace at the new Post Office, Brunswick Square, in 1959. Fred Power had just presented safe-driving awards.

Post office staff at the Strand office following safe-driving awards presented by Cllr Hancock, 1954.

The aftermath of a fire at Dawlish Post Office in the Strand, August 1908.

12
Fire!

Prior to 1900 the only local fire-fighting appliances were owned by insurance companies, who were responsible for attempting to put out fires in the properties of those who were insured with them. No insurance – no help.

The first fire engine in Dawlish was owned by the Sun Insurance Company who bought it for £68 and housed it in Old Town Street. This engine was manually operated and required eleven men to pump on either side while another two directed the jet. Unfortunately, the engine was allowed to deteriorate and by 1899 there was no fire-fighting appliance at all in Dawlish.

Early in 1900 Dawlish bought a steam-engine costing £300 including uniforms and equipment. At an official 'christening' ceremony on the Lawn in April 1900, the new engine was named 'Sir Redvers Buller' after the famous British general who commanded the African and Egyptian campaigns of the 1880s and 1890s and whose statue stands in Exeter.

In those early days, fire fighting was a very primitive affair. The news of the outbreak of fire was brought by someone on a bicycle; the firemen were awakened and hurried to the fire station. The horses would then have to be caught at some distant field and brought back to headquarters where the firemen would set about raising steam on the engine. When they finally reached the fire and connected the hoses from which only a trickle of water flowed, the fire was often out and the place gutted.

By 1930 a motor fire-engine had been bought and this appliance served the town until after the Second World War. Today's fire-service, organised on a county-wide basis, and controlled through the latest technology, is a long way removed from the system of bygone days.

The scene on the Lawn at the official trial and naming of the first Dawlish fire pump, 5 April 1900.

Fire practice on the Lawn, c.1908.

Drawing water from the brook to feed the fire pump during fire practice on the Lawn, c.1908.

Dawlish fire pump, c.1900.

Dawlish firemen pose on the new fire pump, c.1900.

The original Dawlish fire pump following its restoration in September 1914.

Right and below: *Non-standard fire-fighting equipment in use in Dawlish during the Second World War.*

Various items of fire-fighting equipment and the brass plate from the first fire pump in Dawlish, photographed in 1964.

The first motor fire engine in Dawlish, c.1935.

Firemen with a variety of pumps outside Dawlish fire station in 1940.

Now organised as a county-wide service, firemen stand outside Dawlish fire station, 1965.

Scenes from the fire at the Mount Pleasant Inn, 13 August 1955. The fire destroyed six bedrooms, three attic rooms, the kitchen, beer and wine stores, and the lounge and bar with all their fittings. The brigade were called at 1pm but were seriously hampered in fighting the fire by a lack of water pressure. Water had to be pumped from a stream next to Warren Beach Holiday Camp. Six appliances fought the fire, one each from Dawlish and Newton Abbot, and two each from Teignmouth and Torquay.

Above and left: *Scenes at a fire at Langdon Farm on 18 August 1908.*

Below: *Fire at The Cottage, Empson's Hill, 13 April 1911, now the site of Weech House.*

Firemen fight a fire at the cottages, 7 December 1913, near the church entrance where the war memorial now stands.

Fire at Green Cottage, Dawlish Warren, 20 December 1934.

The aftermath of the fire which destroyed Dawlish Warren station, 1924.

On 21 August 1908, just after 1am, the alarm was raised that the Post Office was ablaze. Firemen drew water from the nearby stream and, though the upper storeys were destroyed, the Post Office and Telegraph Office were saved. Fireman Sheppard badly cut a knee during the incident and had it stitched on the spot by Dr Lovely!

On 22 December 1908 Nos 1 and 2 Sea Lawn were gutted by fire, and three people, a lady aged 80 and two young children, tragically died in the blaze.

13
Industrious Dawlish

In common with other towns Dawlish was, in the past, self-sufficient in most things. Food and drink, the manufacture of everyday domestic and agricultural equipment, and the making and repair of cloths and footwear would all have been available locally.

The many grist mills of the area ground corn for local farms and supplied the bakers of the town. The last mill, Knowles', survived well into recent times. Others were sited at Ashcombe, near the school house, another at Weston Mill between Dawlish and Ashcombe, and a third, Torbay Mill, was sited in Brunswick Place.

This last mill is known to have been in situ in 1717, only the huge wheel surviving after its closure in 1959. It was formerly known as Strand Mill, in Mill Row, and the wheel was driven by water that also served Knowles' Mill. From Newhay the water was carried in a leat, via Knowles' Mill, through the top of the Manor Gardens, and along the back of Plantation Terrace to the Strand mill pond.

Knowles' Mill, earlier known as the Town Mills, and earlier still as the Manor Mills, was once owned by a Mrs Tarr whose advertisements read 'Grists Expeditiously Ground'.

At the beginning of the twentieth century there were five forges serving the town. These were Penhaligon's, Chafe's, Noah Knowles', Burch's and Coysh's. Noah Knowles was brother to William, the miller, and his workmen included Jim Mayne, blacksmith, and Tom Davey, wheelwright. The last blacksmith to work at this forge before it closed c.1930, was Robert Frost.

Chafe's forge in Brook Street closed in the early 1900s, while Penhaligon's forge continued into recent times producing traditional wrought iron work.

Brewing was also once an important industry in the town. The Dawlish Brewery supplied many of the local pubs with 'Dawlish Ale'.

Cider too was made, with the Ferris Ellis cider store situated at Houndspool next to the house occupied by Mr H. Whetman, market gardener. From small beginnings in about 1860, the business expanded until in the early 1900s it was producing cider in large quantities from locally grown apples. The product was marketed as 'Dawlish Cider'.

Some years later the business was sold to a Captain Fradgley, and again, in 1932, to Mr Woodgates. The last manager was George Smith who succeeded Bill Knapman. George Powlesland drove the lorry and helped with cidermaking. The stores closed in 1962.

The mill wheel at Brunswick Place.

Top: *Torbay Mill, 1875, formerly known as Strand Mill.*

Above: *Torbay Mill, Brunswick Place, 1912.*

Left: *The mill wheel at Weston Mill, Dawlish Water.*

Right: *The millstones and water-wheel gears at Knowles' Mill, c.1928.*

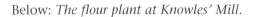

Below: *The flour plant at Knowles' Mill.*

Below: *The boiler room at the Houndspool cider factory, Ashcombe Road, c.1934.*

Below left: *Testing cider from the wooden vats at Houndspool, c.1934.*

Farmer Smith and his son Charlie at the apple press, Lidwell Farm, 1915.

Ashcombe Forge, 1910.

Penhaligon's Forge, Old Town Street, c.1938.

Weech Forge, c.1935.

14
Outings

Social historians will reflect how, at the end of the twentieth century, people moved towards being less gregarious than their forebears. This is due in large part to the independence that car ownership has provided to individuals and families. Why travel with others when you can go alone?

At the advent of motor travel, quite the opposite was true. The invention of the train and, later, the charabanc, meant that people could be transported in large numbers for the first time. This novelty brought a whole new way of enjoying leisure time – the 'outing'.

The following photographs show just how much the novel form of pleasure was indulged, with almost any excuse being given for the chance to travel to new places with friends and colleagues. Private coach businesses developed rapidly on the back of 'day trips' and 'mystery tours', and it was not until cars came within the means of the ordinary family that the public predilection for outings dwindled.

Even before the days of motor transport it was fashionable to take a ride out into the countryside, especially on special occasions such as Bank Holidays. Here members of Dawlish Council stop at Kennford after a trip to visit the Thorns.

A happy group from Dawlish stop at Ashburton following a trip on Dartmoor, 1924.

Regulars of the Devon Arms prepare to set off on an outing organised by Harold Foster, 1924.

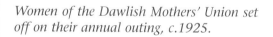

Women of the Dawlish Mothers' Union set off on their annual outing, c.1925.

Dawlish Cricket Club and their followers set off for a game at Wonford, c.1920.

The Conservative Club outing to Tiverton, c.1922.

A Devon Arms outing some time around 1927. In the back of the charabanc is Tommy Shapter 'too drunk to get out for the photograph!'

The Church of England Men's Society members on an outing to Plymouth, via Dartmoor, c.1930.

A Co-operative Society outing organised by Reg Short in 1919.

A Wesleyan Church outing, c.1910.

An outing to Bampton Fair in November 1920.

15
Before the Car Came

The coming of the car brought freedom to travel for ordinary men and women, but it also brought the misery of long traffic jams in summer months in Devon lanes designed for farm carts. Parking in the centre of Dawlish presents residents and visitors alike with problems, cluttering the streets and filling the air with fumes and noise.

It is difficult to imagine that up until the 1930s horse power remained the principal means of transport in and around the town, with most goods and services being delivered by horse and cart. In the early 1900s almost every sizeable back yard held a stable. Horse brakes were used for taking passengers on short trips, parties travelling from Exeter would be waylaid by small boys

waiting at the Warren Copse in the hope of persuading the occupants to part with a few pennies.

Though cars are dangerous today, accidents involving horse-drawn vehicles were also quite common as a newspaper report of June 1898 confirms:

Mr F. G. Webb of Teignmouth Hill, met with a rather severe accident on Saturday afternoon last. Whilst he and his coachman were driving at Langdon, the horse fell, throwing both out of the vehicle. The coachman was not injured, but Mr Webb was less fortunate, and broke his collar bone.

The photographs which follow are reminders of a time when the world was full of horses.

Milk was delivered in a cart carrying churns direct from the dairy. Each day customers would bring out a jug to be filled. Here the milk is delivered in Regent Street, c.1865.

The owner of Langdon House, Mr Parr, is seen here with his coachman, Mr Wilkinson, and daughter, c.1908. The more affluent seldom walked.

Waiting to be loaded is G.B. Avant's haulage van, c.1912. These vehicles were built to travel quite long distances by road.

The Luscombe Estate entry in the cart-horse parade held at Avery's Field, now the playing fields, c.1900.

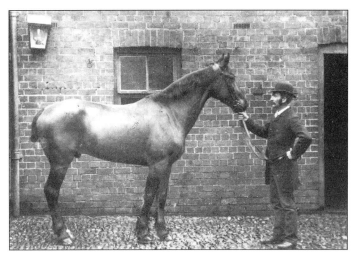

Clockwise from above: *Torbay Mills cart driven by Jack Ware, c.1938; Mr Pearce, who hired out horses, is seen here at the London Hotel Mews in 1875; a hackney carriage picking up customers at the Strand, c.1900; 'Please help our wounded comrades at the Front' – one of the beach donkeys is used to support the fund for horses wounded during the First World War, c.1916.*

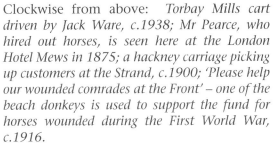

Above: *A cart-horse parade in Dawlish in 1900. Each animal and cart was bedecked with ribbons and polished ornamental brasses, with prizes awarded for the best entries.*

Left: *More serious work for a pair of workhorses at Gatehouse Farm, c.1910.*

Dick Avery with his pony trap at Avery's Field, c.1913.

16
All the Fun of the Fair

You often hear it said that in the 'old days people made their own entertainment', meaning that there were not the multitude of media and other attractions now available to young and old alike. But it is not true to say the public entertainment was entirely absent from the lives of the people of Dawlish in earlier times, and among the greatest attractions was the annual arrival of the travelling fair or circus. In some years four or five different fairs or circuses would visit the town, putting up their 'big top' in the Market Field.

Excitement would mount a week or so in advance of the circus coming to town, with the posting of colourful flyers advertising its arrival. On the day huge steam wagons would descend through the narrow streets, hauling tents and open cages in which wild animals could be glimpsed. Sometimes the arrival would be by train and the station yard would echo to the strange calls of exotic beasts.

In the afternoon the circus performers, usually led by an elephant or two, would parade through the town. Often these great beasts would be taken down on to the beach to bathe, attracting huge crowds.

As the show opened, people streamed along the Exeter Road to the vast marquee, lit by flares and electric lights powered by huge generators that set the evening air abuzz. In 1898 Fourpaw's Great Olympia Circus had a big top with seats for 7000 people, with 150 horses, ponies and mules used to pull their vehicles. In 1903 Bostock & Wombwells Circus came to Dawlish with '700 birds, beasts and reptiles'. Families flocked to watch daring high-wire acts, lion tamers, tigers, bears, wolves and even hyenas.

Modern sensibilities would not stand for such animal acts, but it was not this that upset the townspeople in April 1903, when the *Dawlish Gazette* reported:

Excited schoolchildren follow an elephant that has arrived in town with the circus, c.1905.

The presence of Hancock's steam switchbacks, menagerie, etc. with their blatant organs in a field by the Exeter Road on Good Friday, hurt the religious susceptibilities of many people...'

Those who attended the Saturday performance were treated to additional excitement when a lion escaped, causing panic in the town. The *Gazette* report on the incident throws an interesting light on how the treatment of performing animals was viewed even a century ago, and reflects with credit upon that newspaper's enlightenment.

Providentially the humorous side of the affair is uppermost, in the light of the absence of casualties. But there might have been serious results. To say nothing of the lucky fact that the lion was surprised into cowardice by the novelty of obtaining his freedom. It is a marvel when you think of it that there was no greater personal damage caused by the mad stampede out of the danger zone than manifold bruises and contusions. After all the affair was no joke. While ourselves feeling strongly that such entertainments as these are relics of barbarism that should be unallowable in an enlightened country...'

More scenes at the arrival of the circus, c.1910, with elephants and circus horses being among the major attractions.

The annual visit of the fair to Dawlish was at one time set to coincide with the regatta, this known as Regatta Fair. Other fairs arrived during Easter week and, later, during the first week of August. Before 1930 the booths and rides were set up on the roadway from the station to the Marine Parade, and also where the putting green was later opened in 1930. After this the fair was erected on the site of the Marina car park, but due to the distance from the town fewer people attended. Following the Second World War, Whiteleggs fair was allowed to stand on the Lawn.

Not everyone was happy with the arrival of the circus folk, as the *Gazette* of 22 May 1937 records:

Mr Lamacraft had received a letter from a resident in the Marine Parade with regard to men stripping to the waist in the road for the purpose of washing themselves. If a tent was erected for the purpose there would be no need for them to undress in the road.

The principal attraction of the fairground was the merry-go-rounds, steam driven, with gilded decorations and prancing painted horses. Among the sideshows were 'strong men', 'fat ladies', boxing booths and stalls selling fairings (biscuits), candyfloss and other treats.

Here, c.1920, the helter-skelter towers above the merry-go-round which was driven by the steam engine seen in the middle distance. Those climbing the steps inside the helter-skelter were given a hessian sack or sisal mat on which to descend the spiral slide.

At the time this photograph was taken, around 1890, the fair was erected in York Gardens. In the distance the various tents and rides are being erected.

Swing boats, merry-go-round and helter-skelter draw the crowds at the Regatta Fair, c.1905. The rides were often accompanied by a steam-driven organ playing popular tunes of the day.

Flags bedeck the fairground in this view taken during the 1890s. Note the little cart in the foreground pulled by a goat.

At a penny a ride the helter-skelter (above left) was always popular, as were the swing boats, the latter owned and operated by a family from Exeter. Six to eight youngsters could ride at a time.

All these photographs were taken at the time of the Easter Fair, c.1906.

A dramatic picture of the chair-o-planes in action.

The noise and bustle of the fair is evident from these photographs (left and below), taken c.1905. Hancock's Fair visited around this time, as did Anderton & Rowland's. Later in the twentieth century came Whitelegg's Fair.

Below: *Dawlish Fair, Easter Monday, 1905. Lines of booths were set up along the Strand selling sweets, fairings, winkles, cockles, shrimps and mussels. One of the stalls was kept by Mrs Coombs (she of bathing-machine fame), who sold ginger snaps and 'long comforts' (a type of sweet), helped by her attractive daughter and Fred Salter who later married one another.*

17
Sports and Pastimes

Local sports have long played a large part in the lives of Dawlish people. From football and swimming, to cycling and bowls, the town has a proud record of sporting prowess and self-help achievement in constructing facilities.

This section follows some of these activities through photographs taken over a hundred years or so.

HUNTING

Though not considered a sport by some today, history records that hunting was once a popular activity in Dawlish. The principal pack belonged to the Haldon Harriers who, in the early 1900s, met frequently during the winter months, often in the centre of town. They kept a pack of otter hounds, and also coursed hares, but appear not to have hunted foxes.

A report from the *Dawlish Gazette* of November 1907 records a day in the field:

A splendid day's sport was given in the neighbourhood. A couple of hares were turned out on the marshes at Clog's Hole. Hounds and horses were kept on the go for two hours and seven minutes.

The Haldon Harriers meet at the Grand Hotel, c.1910.

Haldon Harriers meet at the London Hotel, c.1907.

Haldon Harriers at Elm Grove, c.1910.

Hunstmen and hunt followers of the Haldon Harriers meet at the Mount Pleasant Inn, c.1914.

A good turn out of the Harriers at the Royal Hotel, c.1908.

FOOTBALL

For well over a century football has been, and remains, an important activity in the town. The photographs here date from 1897 when Association Football was first started in Dawlish. The first club was formed at a meeting held in the Cosens Institute on 12 September 1897, and the team's first match was against Newton Abbot whom they beat 5–0. They played on a field at Elm Grove Road, and later at Sandy Lane next to what was then Bowerman's sawmills. Games were also played at a field at Reeves Hill where Coronation Avenue now stands.

After an enthusiastic beginning the team waned and by 1906 had ceased. In 1907 it was revived, and by January 1908 the team is recorded as playing its first benefit match in aid of Bill Lambshead who had broken his leg during a junior team match.

And so, over the intervening years, Dawlish has retained a strong link with football in the county, with various clubs representing the town. The following photographs show teams from Dawlish Juniors, Dawlish Argyle, the Magpies and the Chiefs.

Above: Dawlish Juniors, 1910.

Dawlish Chiefs, 1911.

Left: *Dawlish Juniors, 1923.*

Below: *Dawlish Chiefs, League Champions, 1934.*

Left: *Dawlish Second XI, Senior Division II Champions, 1962.*

Below: *First XI, East Devon Senior Cup Winners, 1965.*

CRICKET

Records show that cricket was played at Dawlish from the mid-Victorian period onwards. In September 1899, at the first general meeting of the YMCA, the Dawlish Cricket Club was founded, and in 1912 the club entered the first division of the Exeter & District League.

In recent years the club has played in the Devon League and various other leagues and cups. It has also played under a combined Dawlish and Shaldon team.

The following photographs shows Dawlish teams from the middle decades of the twentieth century in the town.

Above: Dawlish CC v. Constitutional Club, 1939.

Right: Dawlish First XI, 1952.

Dawlish First XI, 1962.

BOWLS

Bowling took place on the Lawn long before the opening of the bowling green on 11 May 1907. Initially there was some disquiet over the building of a green and one such outburst suggested 'the general public would rise in arms at an encroachment for the benefit of the few.' Luckily the event ended without bloodshed and on the opening day the Chairman of Dawlish Town Council, Mr J. Camlin, bowled the inaugural jack, after which a game was played against teams from Exeter and Dawlish, followed by a tea at the Strand Restaurant.

Membership was 2 shillings, kept low in order not to keep 'many working men from joining'. The first captain was Fred Avant and the vice-captain H.S. Loram.

In 1924 a pavilion and clubhouse was built, the money raised by donations, and the Lawn green remained popular with both residents and visitors. In 1935 it was proposed to open another green at the Marina Playing Fields and in May 1940 this was officially opened. Both the town green and Marina have provided endless hours of fun and competition over the years.

Above: *Fred Avant bowling on the Lawn, some time before 1907. At this time the green proper had not been laid down.*

Left: *Members of Dawlish bowling club, c.1908.*

A magnificent photograph of the Lawn bowling green, c.1913.

SWIMMING

From late Victorian times Dawlish was considered one of the leading resorts in the country for the provision of bathing. However, up to the early years of the twentieth century, swimming was a 'men only' pastime, with women's bathing in the sea being confined to a brief and modest dip from a wheeled bathing machine. In contrast, at the male-only preserve of the bathing cove at Coryton, men who did not have costumes bathed in the nude.

Dawlish was one of the first towns in the county to organise swimming matches and in 1864 a Mr F. Davies organised the Dawlish Institute for the Encouragement of Swimming, under which annual competitive matches began. Some idea of the fervour which attended these occasions is given by this contemporary report:

Swimming matches open for public competition are held during the summer months, of which due notice is published in the Dawlish Times. *These occasions are attended with much hilarity, and are very interesting to the visitors. They tend to encourage the useful art of swimming. Every precaution is*

Above: *Fred Holman of Dawlish won a gold medal for the 200 metres breast stroke in the 1908 Olympic Games. Such was the excitement in his native town on hearing the news that cheering crowds assembled in the streets and flags decorated houses and buildings. Holman later became world champion, swimming in an event at the White City stadium in London.*

taken to ensure the safety of those engaged in the competition. A band usually attends.

Well before the end of the century the matches attracted swimmers from Exeter and beyond, and special 'bathing trains' were put on by the GWR. The competition events were held off Early's Wall or the main beach. From this time the names of noted swimmers included David Billington, George Sheppard, Bert Morrish, Frank Goldsworthy, Harry Hartwill, Mark Robins, Percy Dart, Frank Holman and Bert Cornelius.

Of these Fred Holman was the most famous of all, while 'Rock' Goldsworthy won a bet that he could beat the Starcross–Exmouth ferry across the river. He did this by swimming across at half-tide, thus swimming directly across while the ferry had to detour to avoid the sandbanks!

Water polo was also popular, as was a variation known as push ball. The 1920s and '30s also produced a crop of well-known swimmers, including Percy Thorne, Jack West, Fred Denner, Cyril Way, Jim and Jack Burson, Jack Burgess, Archie Bolt and Barlow Morrish.

With the exception of the wartime periods there has always been a swimming club in the town, and sea bathing, along with the indoor swimming pool facilities, provides plenty of opportunity to improve one's skills. Annual galas and other swimming events continue to be held.

Left: *Dawlish water-polo team, c.1900.*

Below: *The push ball team of 1906.*

Dawlish swimmers at the opening season dip, 1933.

Swimmers from Dawlish and Exmouth outside the bathing pavilion, 1933.

Dawlish water-polo team, 1948.

OTHER SPORTS AND GAMES

Hockey, rugby and boxing are among the other sports which Dawlish people have enjoyed to a greater or lesser degree. Golf too has an illustrious history in the town, starting in 1890 when the Rev. Charles Benthall whacked a few balls around the sandy turf of the Warren, culminating in the building of the clubhouse there in 1910.

For the less athletically inclined, darts and snooker have been played in clubs and pubs throughout the town, providing fierce competition in the winter months between various teams in a variety of leagues.

Finally, in this section, boxing is represented as this too enjoyed a brief spell of popularity between 1932 and 1945.

Above: *Dawlish men's hockey team, c.1905.*

Left: *A women's hockey team at Dawlish in 1961.*

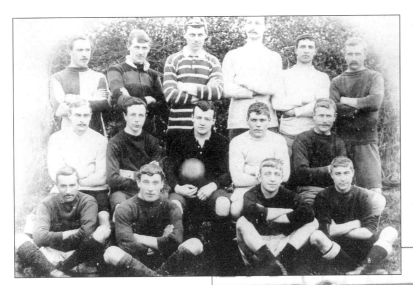

Dawlish rugby team, c.1906.

Below: Mrs Fred Denner opens the putting green for the 1933 season, just three years after it was first opened.

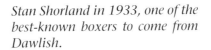

Above: *Dawlish shooting club in 1913, the year in which it won the Morrison Bell cup.*

Stan Shorland in 1933, one of the best-known boxers to come from Dawlish.

Members of the Warren Gold Club at their original clubhouse, 1905.

Below: Bill Morrish in September 1933 with the many trophies he won with his homing pigeons.

Participants in the Chamber of Trade darts final at The Manor, in November 1954, at which the Devon Arms team played a team from the Alexandra Hotel, Starcross.

Players and friends at the Conservative Club snooker championships, 1964.

18
Entertainments

Keeping themselves amused has never been much of a problem for the people of Dawlish. The photographs in this section provide evidence of a wide range of activities under the general heading of entertainment. These range from serious theatrical productions to pantomime, from opera to carnivals, and of course the cinema.

The repertory theatre company in Dawlish first played to audiences in the 1950s, initially using the secondary school hall, then later moving to the famous Hut – a draughty ex-Army hut that did great service as the centre of entertainment for the town. In the late 1950s the repertory company purchased the Shaftesbury Hall and, after a great deal of effort, opened it as a theatre seating 170 in 1959. This became the focus for theatrical productions, including opera.

Pantomime, dancing and amateur dramatics were once held in the Assembly Rooms and the Hut. These productions brought people of the town together – as they still do – and provided an outlet for those with less serious intentions in the theatre.

Permanent cinema in Dawlish dates back to 1911 when Walford's cinema opened in Chapel Street. The Scala was opened in the late 1920s and ran until 1960, but in between times a variety of venues were used to show films as the photograph below, showing crowds waiting in Lansdowne Place to see a film at the Vestry Hall, illustrates.

THE SILVER SCREEN

Coming to the corner stood a long, low building, the picture house, the dear little Scala cinema. I believe it is a printing business now – what a shame. Oh the delights and pleasures of the silver screen at the little Scala. Many happy memories of the heyday of films seen there, afternoon and evening performances, the Saturday Matinee was very popular. A really charming gentleman was the Manager, a Mr Payne. He was tall and thin and always dressed in an evening suit and greeted everyone as old friends. After paying our pennies or shillings at the tiny cubicle in the little foyer, Mr Payne ushered us into our seats like royalty. He would say to the kiosk lady, 'one lady and her dog, 1 ticket only' as for some reason my mother often took our dog Tony to see the show and he sat on her lap and seemed to enjoy the film as much as we did. He was such an intelligent little terrier and much loved, and no one strangely enough thought it odd when we all marched into the ninepenny seats, dog and all.

PIN UPS AND CHIPS

We usually tried to sit half way from the screen, well away from the foot-stamping, noisy youngsters who liked the front seats where they could whistle and boo during drawn-out love scenes and cheer and stamp during cowboy films. But if they made too much noise and other customers were getting fed up with them spoiling the film, the film would be stopped, the lights go on, and down would march Mr Payne, very stern and wrathful. He would evict the worst ringleaders who usually managed to slip back through side doors in the interval as the doors would be opened slightly for some fresh air, and to let some of the wreathing blue cigarette smoke out.

It was always a long programme in which you enjoyed glamour, escapism and adventure for a few hours, usually in the welcome company of friends or family. Topics of conversation for days afterwards centred on discussion of your particular idols and 'pin ups' of the day. The first film shown was a short minor supporting film, then an interval, next a lengthy newsreel by Pathe News, then various local adverts and clips of films to come and last of all, the major film. We did not have pocket money then and saving our pennies for the cinema delights was hard work. Everyone stood patriotically at the end for the National Anthem, silent, arms to sides, no furtive fumbling to get your coats and scarves, or people quietly sliding out while it was being played. If we were in funds, heads full of the film and its glamorous unattainable stars, eyes sore from the clouds of cigarette smoke, we would queue up at a little fish and chip shop which was on a steep hill on our way home. Walking home and holding in cold hands the cones of newspaper with hot fat, deliciously vinegary chips and sometimes battered cod, eating it all with our fingers, it made the walk home go much faster, especially in blackout days in the war.

A production by the Dawlish Pantomime Company in 1934, Babes in the Wood.

The cast and chorus of Robinson Crusoe, *also by the Dawlish Pantomime Company, 1936.*

Above left: *Cyril Shorland and Joan Petherick and* (right) *Nan Sampson and Beryl Hartwill, in* Aladdin, *December 1937.*

Above left: *Phyllis Warren as Aladdin in 1937 and* (right) *Harry Hartwill and Charlie Coombs in* Babes in the Wood, *1939.*

Top left: The Shaftesbury Theatre under construction in 1959.

Scenes from various repertory company productions, clockwise from above: Who Goes There, Twelfth Night, *and* See How They Run.

Early operatics in Dawlish included this production of Miss Hook of Holland *by the Amateur Light Operatic Company at the Scala in 1929.*

The Pirates of Penzance *at the Shaftesbury Theatre, performed by the Dawlish Musical Society in 1960.*

The Mikado *at the Shaftesbury Theatre, performed by the Dawlish Musical Society in 1964.*

Scenes from Dawlish carnivals over the years.

Left: *Entries for the Queen of Carnival contest, 1933.*

Below: *'Filling the new tank' - a reference to the newly-built reservoir, 1937.*

Below: *Carnival collectors with a barrel organ, 1927.*

Right: *Carnival revellers in 1925.*

19
Schooldays

The National Parochial School was established in Old Town Street in 1819 funded by government grant, local subscriptions and 'children's pence'. In 1869 there were 130 pupils, 90 boys and 40 girls, under the tutelage of Mr W. Towill and Miss Beavan.

In later years a new boys' school was built higher up the hill to accommodate over 200 pupils. The first entry in the log-book is dated 1863 and at this time the school was in the charge of Mr Chinneck. The infants and girls remained at the Old Town Street school which was enlarged in 1898.

In 1937 the schools were divided into infant and junior co-educational establishments, the infants remaining in Old Town Street, while all children over the age of eight attended the boys' school. In the same year a county secondary school was built at Elm Grove Road and all pupils over the age of eleven were transferred there, or to the grammar school in Teignmouth.

In 1939–40 some of the village schools in the area were closed and children brought into Dawlish by bus. With schools enlarged, more bussing takes place today than ever before, with a huge migration of children to and from Dawlish each day.

A number of private schools have existed in Dawlish over the years. In 1869 Miss Cotton's school was listed at Cleveland Place, while Misses Young and Hance held school at Haldon Terrace. Others have been Lanherne's boarding school for girls, Clyde House school, St Timothy's preparatory school, Cleveland House school, Mrs Rippington's, Mrs Lambshead's, Miss Rowe's and Miss Cole's Park Road school, and Miss Mackenzie's Sidford school.

Dawlish boys' school in 1904. Mr Lamacraft is the young master on the right.

Dawlish infants, 1906. Note the pinafore dresses worn by the girls and the starched collars of some of the boys. It was not unusual at this time for younger boys to be dressed in their older sister's hand-me-down clothes.

Boys at Dawlish Board School, c.1905. Board Schools were the forerunners of state-funded schools.

A classroom interior at Truman Hall, Cleveland House school, c.1932. Note the teacher's desk facing the pupils' wooden benches.

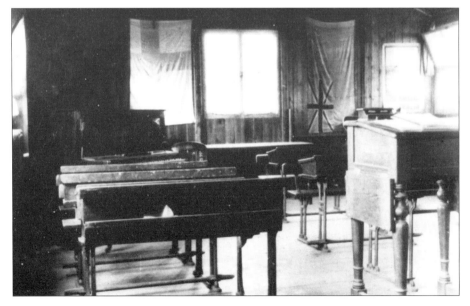

Dawlish boys' school, 1908.

Ashcombe School, c.1920. At this time most villages had their own schools, often partly funded by subscription and by the children's own payment of a penny or so per day.

Dawlish boys' school, 1922. By this date it was described as the Council School, as chalked on the football held by the boy in the centre.

A class of mixed ages at Cockwood village school, c.1900. Such small establishments as this would have had one qualified teacher and a pupil-teacher, often a former attendee of the school.

Dawlish boys' school. The teachers are Headmaster, Jimmy King (left), and George Staddon (right).

Pupils and staff from Cleveland House school on the beach at the Warren, 1932.

Mrs Lambshead's private school, Dawlish, c.1930.

Staff at Dawlish girls' school, c.1934. Clockwise from back row left: Miss Flynn, Miss Hinton, Miss Wooley, Miss Cox, Mrs Rowley, Miss Richards, Miss Wilkinson (later Mrs Williams).

Dawlish boys' school, 1934.

Dawlish girls' school, 1923.

A mixed group of children from the boys' and girls' school holding up their war savings books, c.1917.

20
Church and Chapel

Little remains of the former church that stood on the site of the present parish church of St Gregory. Rebuilt in 1824, only the Perpendicular red tower is ancient. Much interior work has been carried out since that date and the east window of stained glass is particularly fine. In 1873 the triple-decker pulpit was removed during major work on the interior during which the floor was lowered and the seats renewed.

In 1889 the organ was renewed at a cost of £1000, and in 1895 work again began on alterations including the removal of the galleries and the restoration of the nave. In 1911 two more bells were added to the peal of six in commemoration of the coronation of George VI.

St Mark's Church, or chapel of ease, was built under the hand of Charles Hoare who, along with his wife, is commemorated in two stained-glass windows.

St Agatha's Roman Catholic Church in Exeter Road was completed in 1909. Before this date the Catholic community held their services in a room at the Grand Hotel.

Nonconformity was strong in the West Country and in Dawlish too. Among the various chapels and other places of worship that sprang up to meet the needs of these vigorous groups was the Independent Chapel, said to have been built in Chapel Street in 1814. In 1870 the congregation purchased the York Inn situated in the Strand, demolished it, and in its place built the Congregational church in Gothic style.

The Wesleyans laid the foundation stone of the Methodist chapel in Brunswick Place. Built at a cost of £1000, Ebenezer Pardon was, along with Messrs Bowden and Brock, a chief contributor to its cost. It was opened in 1861.

The Salvation Army too has a firm tradition in Dawlish. The Dawlish Corps was formed in 1887 and opened by Major John Roberts in October of that year. The present chapel was built in 1881, then used by the Primitive Methodists. The 'Tin Tabernacle' as it became known, was taken over by the Salvation Army in 1936.

The parish church of St Gregory photographed some time before 1875. In 1897 extensive alterations were carried out both to the interior and exterior of the building.

These two photographs, the top one taken before 1880, the lower one c.1910 following restoration in 1897, show the stark differences in the fabric of the building.

Similar drastic changes can be seen by comparing these two photographs of the interior of St Gregory's, the left one taken before 1873 and the one on the right in 1953. In the older picture the original box pews and the triple-decker pulpit can be seen.

The ruins of ancient Lidwell Chapel are associated with the legend of an evil monk who waylaid travellers on Haldon.

The two new bells that were added to the peal of six at St Gregory's to celebrate the coronation of King George VI.

Bell ringers at St Gregory's, c.1902. The small boy is Wilf Gay, son of George Gay second from right.

Schoolboys pose in the parish stocks for this postcard photograph in St Gregory's churchyard.

Dawlish cemetery and mortuary chapel built in 1883–84, and shown here c.1890.

The cemetery and mortuary chapel, c.1900.

The altar in a room at the Grand Hotel, c.1909, where Roman Catholics attended services before the Catholic church was built.

The combined choirs of St Mark and St Gregory outside the parish church following the coronation thanksgiving ceremony 1953.

Above and right: *Baptism in the sea. One at Cockwood, c.1930, and that on the right at Dawlish main beach in May 1957, performed by the Rev. Leslie Partridge.*

An open-air service on the beach conducted by members of the Christian Brethren, May 1957.

The induction of the vicar of Dawlish, the Rev. John Delve, by the Bishop of Crediton in 1955.

The dedication of the war memorial at Holcombe Church, c.1919.

A united service was held in the open air on a Lawn air-raid shelter on VJ Day, 1945. The service was conducted by the Rev. G. S. Trewin, and the lesson read by Pilot Officer Geoff Cowling.

Members of the Salvation Army in Dawlish, c.1932.

21
Dawlish on Parade

In 1852 when Britain and France were enemies facing one another across the narrow English Channel, a Dr John Bucknill, then Superintendent of Exminster Hospital, formed the Devon Rifle Volunteers. Their motto was 'defence not defiance'. Although initially funded from private sources, in 1872 the government instituted training camps under Regular Army instruction. Here the men learnt weapons training and were drilled into a disciplined force. Musketry practice was held at the Warren, and later a rifle range was built at Starcross.

Early in the twentieth century the Company was commanded by a Captain Waterfield. Buglers in smart uniforms were seen about the town blowing 'dress for parade', at which the Company would fall in outside the drill hall in Manor Row. The drill hall was situated next to the old Manor Inn in Brook Street.

When the Territorial Army was formed in 1908, the Volunteers were disbanded. All those who wished to continue service were absorbed into the Prince of Wales Battalion which fought with distinction in the Great War.

At the outset of the Second World War, many Dawlish men again found themselves in uniform and those who were too old to serve were enlisted in the Local Defence Volunteers, later to become the Home Guard. The first serving member in Dawlish was Ernie Fewings, who signed on at the police station a few seconds before his colleagues Ben Hutchings and Bill Back.

While these men trained to repel any invaders, other Dawlish men and women served in the forces in all theatres of war. The names of those who fell in their defence of the kingdom are now recorded on the war memorials in the district.

The 5th Devons Bugle Band including a number of men from Dawlish, at Newton Abbot, c.1905. The extreme youth of some of the boys seen in the photograph was not unusual for those times.

Left: *The last Church Parade of H Company, the Devon Rifle Volunteers, and members of the Coast Guard Service, under Chief Officer Lewis; Captain Waterfield commanding, 1907.*

Below: *H. Company commanded by Captain Woolacott, 1901.*

Left: *Dawlish Territorials in camp, 1913.*

Below: *Dawlish men on leave from Salisbury Plain before being shipped to India, 1914.*

The landlord and landlady of the Red Lion, Mr and Mrs Downing, c.1914, with men believed to be of the 8th Devons, who were billeted in the Bartons.

A tension bridge built by the men of the Devon & Somerset Engineers as a military exercise. The top of Teignmouth Hill, from Lea Mount to West Cliff, was joined by a footbridge and a transport bridge.

The 1st Devon & Somerset Engineers on exercise, in 1907, at the bridge on Lea Mount.

More exercises for the 1st Devon & Somerset Engineers in August 1907. Here they are building a pontoon bridge at Coryton, using beer barrels for buoyancy.

Dawlish Territorials encamped on Salisbury Plain, 1910.

The 1st Devon & Somerset Engineers on a hot August day in 1907 are building trenchworks on exercise at Blackdown. Useful work, as but a few years later many of them would be building trenches with a real purpose in the mud of Flanders.

Above: *Dawlish Territorials, 1921.*

Left: *British prisoners of war with their German captors, c.1916. George Casely of Dawlish is seen immediately behind the man sitting on the barrel.*

Dawlish Home Guard, c.1940. Sergeant F. Key with his section, photographed in the infants' school yard.

A full Company of Dawlish Home Guard, c.1940, with Lieutenants Hutchings and Cornelius.

Everyone was very conscientious over blackout materials over windows and doors. If a bit of light showed, the ARP Warden soon knocked at your door. Cars had strips of paper covering most of their lights, the same with torches, so only a glimmer of light showed. Gardens were dug over to grow more vegetables and keep chickens, we had both, so we were not short of food, though my mother would never kill any of the hens, they were Rhode Island Reds, lovely layers. They all had names and came out to have their backs stroked. One favourite was called Henrietta, and she knew her name.

Mother became an Air Raid Warden with tin hat and stirrup pump and my father, an old soldier from the First World War, joined the Home Guard. In the early days of the war they used to make us laugh at their antics. Before they had proper uniforms and rifles to use in their exercises they had to use broom handles for rifles, black their faces with soot (the rest of the soot went into the vegetable plot), and throw flour bombs at each other, mainly around Dawlish Brook and gardens. But apart from the laughter they were nearly all old soldiers and would have given a good account of themselves very bravely if called into action because of invasion.

From top: *British planes fly over the Warren in 1939. Members of Dawlish Rescue & Demolition Corps, c.1942. A Home Guard unit formed into 'Haldon Commandos' in preparation for possible enemy landings on Haldon Moor. They were trained in explosives, specialising in the laying of mines and also in demolition.*

A remarkable sequence of photographs taken in 1943 following the crash landing near Dawlish of an American Air Force B17F Flying Fortress on 27 January 1943. Nicknamed 'Werewolf' by its crew, based at Molesworth, Hants, the plane got into difficulties following a raid on the German submarine pens at Brest. Hit by flak, the plane lost two engines, and a third began to lose power.

Pilot, First Lieutenant George Oxrider, ordered his crew to bale out and then with great skill and daring landed his plane in a large field near Langdon Hospital. The plane was only slightly damaged and engineers decided to fit three new engines and fly her out.

Some weeks later, with the new engines fitted, and a rough grass runway laid out, the plane was flown off by a new crew. Lieutenant Oxrider was decorated for his bravery but was killed later in the war.

PLANES OVER DAWLISH

Gun pillboxes, ack-ack guns, Nissen huts, sprang up all along the Lady's Mile, and even took over our little wood we used to play in. Most of the beaches were closed off with barbed-wire defences, but some parts were left open for people to bathe and enjoy the beach. We witnessed German bombs and fighter planes going up the Exe Estuary to bomb poor Exeter, and you could see from Dawlish, the red glow in the sky from raids on Plymouth and Devonport docks. I saw two dogfights over the estuary and sea, one enemy plane spiralling down in flames into the sea while a Spitfire did a victory roll. I believe several plane wrecks have been recovered from the bay and were exhibited at an Air Museum somewhere near Totnes. We had the odd stray bomb from bombers finishing off their load of bombs, and one American Flying Fortress landed, damaged, just outside Dawlish, near a home for handicapped children. My younger brother and I cycled out to view the plane in awe before a convoy of military and airforce vehicles came with spares to get her airborne again, which was quite a job.

Left: Women played a vital role in the war effort and none more so than nurses. Here members of the Dawlish Red Cross are seen on a VAD (Voluntary Aid Detachment) training course at Osborne some time before the war.

Below: A 'Wings for Victory' parade on the Strand, 26 April 1943. Such schemes were initiated in order to encourage the amount of money subscribed to National Savings. A parade and display of military equipment often accompanied these fund-raising events.

EVACUEES

We had various evacuees in Dawlish at one time or another, a particularly nice family evacuated from London, while the husband, a dentist, stayed on with his practice in their London home. The Robertsons, his wife and two children, Eileen and Derek, bought a second home just up the road from our house. Eileen joined my class at the Teignmouth Grammar School, great company for me. She loved horse riding and was a competent horse rider and taught me to ride. She would hire a massive brown horse called Captain, a very amiable horse, while I had to cycle to a local farm, and catch and saddle a rather temperamental pony called Pixie. We would ride all over the country lanes, up to Haldon and sometimes to Dawlish Warren. There was very little traffic on the roads, only increasing with army vehicles etc., as the war went on and building up to D-Day.

In Dawlish I do not think many people had proper air-raid shelters. Most, like us, relied on sitting under the stairs or a big table, or going down to cellars when the sirens went. As the war went on, platoons of soldiers would be drilled in the little side road opposite us, by the Rockstone Hotel. My mother used to feel sorry for them, as one particular Sergeant really bawled and shouted at them and even in winter had them drilling without tunics or shirts on. If I was home we would make two huge kettles of cocoa, as we were not short of milk, and spare what little bit of sugar from our rations we could to go in the cocoa. At a respite in the drilling, off we would go, mother with the kettles and myself with a tray with an assortment of mugs and cups. The soldiers were so grateful for the hot drinks, even the Sergeant, poor young fellows. I wonder if any survived to remember a lady's kindness with hot drinks, in the war.

Above: *The huge relief at the war's end was met with a huge public wave of celebration. Here the residents of Albert Place celebrate with a victory tea, May 1945.*

Left: *A victory tea celebration in the High Street, May 1945.*

22
People and Personalities from the Past

Every community throws up those people who seem larger than life. Perhaps it is because such people have made good, become 'somebody' in local life, or perhaps it is simply because they stand out from the crowd. There is a general complaint that modern society has less time for individuality. It is certainly true that in the past, in small communities such as Dawlish, everyone knew everyone else, and eccentric behaviour was tolerated, even encouraged, rather than being frowned upon.

Family names associated with the town include Annetts, Allen, Avant, Avery, Back, Blackmore, Bolt, Boone, Bowden, Brimble, Brock, Burch, Burdick, Burgess, Butler, Capener, Camlin, Chapman, Cheetham, Coleman, Cook, Cornelius, Cox, Cridge, Crook, Cross, Curtis, Davey, Delve, Dyble, Eardley, Everleigh, Ferris, Fey, Foster, Fox, Gibbings, Gilbert, Goodridge, Hanock, Harris, Hatcher, Hill, Hobden, Hole, Holman, Hopkins, Hutchings, King, Knapman, Knight, Knighton, Lake, Lamacraft, Lambshead, Lear, Lewis, Loram, Love, Manley, Marham, Maunder, Merritt, Moore, Morrish, Muncey, Nicholls, Patrick, Payne, Peck, Penhaligon, Peyton, Reeves, Richards, Riley, Roberts, Robins, Ross, Rowle, Sage, Sampson, Saundry, Scott, Shapter, Shelston, Shorland, Short, Simkin, Slee, Stone, Talbut, Tarr, Thomas, Tozer, Trant, Trewin, Way, Westenra, Williams, Wreford and Yelland.

In the photograph albums compiled by Bernard Chapman there is a section on local personalities – people who had made their mark in the town, for whatever reason. As Mr Chapman makes clear: 'All the characters are, or were, well known in the town, and those who have been left out are excluded simply because no photographs exist.' Nor is there any explanation given for their inclusion: 'No attempt has been made to describe the personalities, such a task would produce only personal opinion...'. In this section are just a few of the many photographs collected by Mr Chapman.

Bill Dart. A cry of 'fresh fish' or 'Dawlish mackerel' brought his customers out into the street.

Mrs Stab (Brixham Kit) and Mr Main. Mrs Stab's cry was 'Hake, Dabs and Whiting'.

Charlie Cornelius.

'Greybird' Alfred Mathews.

Courtenay Marshall, 'Old Marshall', whose cry of 'All vull o't', was well known to newspaper readers.

Frank and Jack Dart

Sam Murch – the 'Okey Pokey Man'.

Tommy Shapter (see page 87).

Ernest 'Mac' Yelland.

William 'Charlie' Chaplin.

Charlie Coombs.

Len Trant.

Rosalie Hacon.

Mary Margaret Charlotte Avant Washington.

Kit Mitchell and Annie Lambshead.

King 'Slingey' Briscoe.

Jack Richards Snr.

From left: *Cecil and Reg Hopkins, Ernest Yelland.*

William Williams.

William Jeffrey of Ashcombe. Born in Chagford in 1866, he moved to Langdon Barton Farm and lived to be 100 years of age

William Trant with shotgun and terriers outside his West End shop.

Pat Boone.

Ernie Cotton (see page 29).

Lewis Trant.

Characters from a farce 'Paddy and the Ghost' which was part of an entertainment given by the Dawlish Black Diamonds in the Sergeants' Mess of the Devon and Somerset Engineers (see page 133). Pictured left to right are S. Knapman as the ghost, P.C. Harris, W.H. Narramore and J.H. Lamacraft.

23

The Warren and Beyond

Once the haunt of smugglers, by 1902 Dawlish Warren was described as an 'exclusive hamlet', and the residents there were complaining at the prospect of the golf course being built. By 1905 a new railway halt had been built so that day trippers from Exeter could stop off at the Warren to swim and picnic.

More and more development took place, with little wooden bungalows springing up across the Warren throughout the 1930s, until post-war planning regulations became more stringent. The war and winter gales put an end to many of these makeshift buildings and, by the early 1960s, only one of them remained.

Since the 1950s there has been a gradual development of the Warren as a holiday resort, with chalets, caravan parks, camp grounds and shops all built to cater for the tourist.

In recent years much conservation work has been carried out, not only to protect the Warren from erosion by the sea and by humans, but also to preserve the flora and fauna of this important coastal habitat.

This section contains a number of photographs showing the Warren as it used to be, and takes us to nearby Cockwood, once best known for its famous cockles.

A view across the Warren from the Warren Halt bridge, c.1910.

A VISIT TO THE WARREN

When I was about 10 years old, about 1932, some friends asked me to visit a relation of theirs, who lived for the summer months in an upside-down converted boat, in the middle of the dunes. It was wonderful, just like the little boat house Ham lived in when David Copperfield visited it with Peggotty in the story by Charles Dickens. A very snug little living room, with a tiny fireplace and chimney, oil lamps, and a ladder at the side of the room leading up to two tiny bedrooms, with little windows cut out of the bottom of the boat, which now formed the roof. We had a lovely tea, and how I would have loved to stay there on holiday, to wake up to the sound of gulls and have the sands and sea right on the doorstep – we did envy them. Walking home, we usually went over the railway bridge, where on a siding were two converted railway coaches, where two families lived permanently, and on up to the Lady's Mile. Before we crossed to the path there were three little chalet bungalows on a grassy area with lovely wild lupins and gorse bushes in the gardens.

The Mount Pleasant Inn on the Warren, c.1900.

The original Warren tea rooms and restaurant, c.1910.

A view across the Warren from the entrance, July 1932. In the far background is the Warren Restaurant, advertising teas, lunches and refreshments. Visitors' cars are lined up in the foreground, close to the little shack which sells teas and toffee.

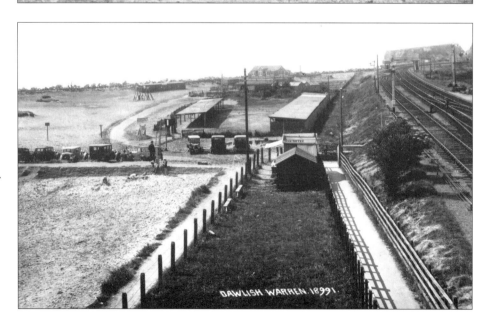

A view across the Warren taken c.1875. At this time almost no development had taken place. The old wooden bridge can just been seen centre left in the photo.

The old wooden bungalows on the Warren, built during the 1920s and '30s, were erected on stilts to keep them above high tides.

By the 1940s many of the bungalows had succumbed to the tides of time, and nature. On the right of this photograph, taken c.1938, a concrete cesspit from one of the ruined bungalows lies at the water's edge.

By 1964, when this photograph was taken, only one of the bungalows remains. This too was destroyed by high seas not long after.

The Warren golf course showing the old Round House which became ruinous during the late 1940s.

Warren Beach, 1938.

Ladies playing on the Warren golf course, c.1910.

One of the early facilities for summer visitors to the Warren, c.1935, a badminton court situated just north of Dawlish Warren station.

COCKWOOD

A view across to Cockwood, c.1900. It is actually made up of three hamlets, Cockwood, Middlewood and Westwood. At high tide the water laps the harbour wall at the Anchor Inn, and swans swim around the railway arch. In summer cars bring chaos to the narrow lanes but in early days this little community was engaged in fishing and, in particular, with the ancient occupation of cockle-raking. This industry was undertaken exclusively by women who wore large 'bloomers', pants into which they tucked their dresses in order to keep them out of the mud. Straw bonnets were also worn, kept on the head by a scarf tied under the chin.

The Anchor Inn at Cockwood, c.1880.

Cockwood cockle rakers, c.1910.

The Dodge family outside their cottage in Cockwood, c.1916. The area was well known for its market-garden produce, to which the marrows heaped in this photograph testify.

The estate of Cofton, which is associated with Cockwood and provides the village with a church, is mentioned in a deed of 1270. At the start of the nineteenth century the church was in ruins until it was restored by the Earl of Devon in 1839.

Subscribers

Frances G. Annett, Dawlish, Devon

Mrs D. Annetts, Dawlish, Devon

Sarah Annetts and Marc Brooks, Exeter, Devon

Ashcombe Village Club, Ashcombe, Devon

Mr and Mrs R. G. Beasley

Anthony Black and Sarah Purnell, Dawlish, Devon

David Blackham, Dawlish, Devon

Wendy Boland, Dawlish, Devon

Roy B. S. Bolt, Dawlish, Devon

Edward Bolt, Dawlish, Devon

The Boneham Family, Dawlish, Devon

Richard William Boyne, Dawlish, Devon

Brendan and Nicola, Coastguards Bistro, Dawlish, Devon

Jesse Bridge

Carole and Jim Britton, Dawlish, Devon

Ian Brooks, Dawlish, Devon

Montague and Kathleen Brooks, Dawlish, Devon

Simon R. Broom, Port Road, Dawlish, Devon

M.J., M.M., and S.M. Brown, Burnley, Lancs.

Mike, Ruth, Hayley and Jenna Brown, Dawlish, Devon

Martin Burdick, Shaldon, Devon

Rosamund and John Burley, Treston Close, Dawlish, Devon

Joan and Graham Burley, West End Avenue, Harrogate, Yorkshire

K. J. Burrow, Bucks Cross, Devon

Dinah C. Butt, Dawlish, Devon

Bob and Aileen Callender, Dawlish, Devon

Mrs A. M. (Dill) Cameron, Dawlish, Devon

Cynthia Rose Campbell, Dawlish, Devon

Margaret and John Camus, Dawlish, Devon

Nicholas Chandler, Dawlish, Devon

John C. Charlett, Dawlish, Devon

Miss Juliet E. Chenery, Hazelwood Park, Dawlish Warren, Devon

Mr Ron Clark, Dawlish, Devon

Michael Clayson and Robert Vickery, Dawlish, Devon

Mr Michael J. Cobbett

Valerie L. Cockram, Dawlish, Devon

M. Cockram, Wells

Bill and Jean Cockram, Dawlish, Devon

Violet Cook, Dawlish, Devon

Fay and Steven Corbett, Surbiton, Surrey

Roger F. Course, Dawlish, Devon

Malvine S. Crugten

Simon and Aiden Curl, Dawlish, Devon

Peggy Curle, Dawlish, Devon

Mrs Julia P. Curtis, Dawlish, Devon

Brian Davis, Winterbourne, South Gloucestershire

J. Day, Dawlish, Devon

Derick A. Drake, Dawlish Warren, Devon

Christopher J. Duckworth, Dawlish, Devon

Mrs Elizabeth K. Elford, Clutton, Som.

Doreen E. Elgood, Dawlish, Devon

Dr R. Elliott, Dawlish, Devon

Mr D. D. Evans, Dawlish, Devon

Mr Lee D. Evans, Dawlish, Devon

Sandra and John Evans, Dawlish, Devon

Ian Ferguson, Holcombe

David Force, Dawlish, Devon

Don and Sylvia Forrow, Dawlish, Devon

Mrs B. French and Mr B. P. Tugwell, Dawlish, Devon

Barrie Frost, Dawlish Community College

Tony and Thelma Fryer, Dawlish, Devon

Lauren Louise Gibbins, Dawlish, Devon

Joanna and Richard Gibson, Dawlish Water, Devon

Sheila and Paul Gibson, Dawlish Water, Devon

R. J. R. Gibson, Sydney, Australia

Prof W. P. R. Gibson AM, Sydney, Australia

Mrs Joyce Gillespie, Dawlish, Devon

Joan Glenny, Dawlish, Devon

Andrew Goodridge, Dawlish, Devon

Rita C. D. Graves, Dawlish, Devon

Julie A. Green, Dawlish, Devon

Kay Patricia Hammond, Broadstairs, Kent

Roy and Sandra Hancock, Dawlish, Devon

Norman and Carol Hardyman, Dawlish, Devon

Mr Graham Harvey,

John Haynes, Dawlish, Devon

Thomas R. and Linda M. Haynes, Dawlish, Devon

John Hedley Way, Dawlish, Devon

Robert and Jane Hill, Teignmouth, Devon

Ian D. P. Hill, Dawlish, Devon

Doug and Margaret Hislop, Dawlish, Devon

Michael Hogg, Dawlish, Devon

Mike and Eileen Holcombe, Dawlish, Devon

Bryan R. Holman, Dawlish, Devon

Roy H, Holman, Dawlish, Devon

Tom Hunt, Ashcombe, Devon

Mo Hutchings, Dawlish, Devon

Barbara and Chris Janes, Dawlish, Devon

George Jeffery, Cofton, Devon

Eric Jolly, The Summer House, Dawlish, Devon

Ruth Jones (née Ireland), Dawlish, Devon

Derrick M. Kent, Dawlish, Devon

Mr T. H. Kernick, Dawlish, Devon

Audrey M. King, Dawlish, Devon

Joan L. Knox, Dawlish, Devon

Peter and Sarah Lamb, Dawlish, Devon

Miss Violet R. M. Lambshead, Overbrook, Dawlish, Devon

Daniel Langdale, Dawlish, Devon

David B. Langrish, Salisbury

Peter Larkman, Dawlish, Devon

Priscilla Lawley, Dawlish, Devon

Oliver Le Cheminant and Rebecca Young, Holcombe Village, Devon

Dr Don Leader, Dawlish, Devon

Michael Leat

Mr Lance John Loram,

Olive P. Loram, Dawlish, Devon

Nolan J. Lovell, Dawlish, Devon

Mrs Kathleen Lundmark, Calgary,
  Alberta, Canada
Ray and Cynthia Maidment, West Sussex
Nick and Chrissy Marks, Poppyfields,
  Dawlish, Devon
Mrs Eleanor Marshall, Pitsford,
  Northamptonshire
Jan and Kelvin Martin, Dawlish, Devon
Dr and Mrs Martinsen-Tugwell,
  Stavanger, Norway
Alan Mason, Dawlish, Devon
Bill McAlister, Dawlish, Devon
Mr and Mrs M. McCutchion, Dawlish,
  Devon
James McFarlane, Dawlish, Devon
Sylvia Barclay McKechnie, Dawlish,
  Devon
Denise McMahon, Dawlish, Devon
Ann P. Melleney, Dawlish, Devon
Gerald P. Miles, Dawlish, Devon
Bryan Millerchip, Edward Street,
  Nuneaton, Warks.
Irene Mitchell, Dawlish, Devon
Georgina C. Moore, Dawlish, Devon
Norman I. Morris, Dawlish, Devon
Sheila Morrish-Stevens, Dawlish, Devon
John Parkin, Dartmouth and Dawlish
Pat and Tony, West Cliff Road, Dawlish,
  Devon
Chris Pattle, Dawlish, Devon
Desmond Pike, Dawlish, Devon
Mr Ronald L. Pluck, Ashburton, New
  Zealand
T. Pool, Ilsington, Devon
John and Joy Pring, Dawlish, Devon
Elizabeth Anne Reed (née Boyne),
  Dawlish, Devon

John and Penny Richardson, Dawlish,
  Devon
B. M. Roberts, Dawlish, Devon
Mr Ralph G. Rogers, Dawlish, Devon
Georgina and Eleanor Rowse, Dawlish,
  Devon
Ian Sanders, Exeter, Devon
Betty Saulsbury, Dawlish, Devon
Joan Saunders (née Butler), High Street,
  Dawlish, Devon
John and Christine Seaborne, Dawlish,
  Devon
Eileen and Mick Selley, Dawlish, Devon
Tony Shapter, Three Beaches, Paignton,
  Devon
Ralph John Sharland, Dawlish, Devon
J. R. Shephard, Plymouth, Devon
Brigette R. Shorland, Dawlish, Devon
Fay Shorland, Dawlish, Devon
Maurice W. Shorland, Dawlish, Devon
Brian W. Shorland, Dawlish, Devon
Nicholas C. Simpson, Deputy District
  Judge. Roadwater, Somerset.
Eric Simpson DPA, Dawlish, Devon
C. R. G. Slack, Dawlish, Devon
Dr S. W. Smith and Mrs R. S. Annetts-
  Smith, Epsom, Surrey
Leonard H. Stening, Dawlish, Devon
Barry R. Stickland, Dawlish, Devon
Lesley J. Sudwell, Dawlish, Devonshire
Mike Swift, Dawlish, Devon
Eve Sykes, Dawlish, Devon
Robert and Carole Tapper, Bristol
Lt Col. and Mrs Charles Teall, Holcombe,
  Dawlish, Devon
Mr and Mrs Thomas, Luton
Rachel and Jon Tibbetts, Dawlish, Devon

S. and B. Tindal, Dawlish, Devon

Peter J. Tucker, Dawlish, Devon

Austin Turner, Cleave, Dawlish, Devon

Michael J. Varvel, Dawlish, Devon

Brian and Gillian Vickery,

Joyce A. L. Voysey, New Malden, Surrey

John F. W. Walling, Newton Abbot, Devon

Martin Way, Churchill Avenue, Dawlish, Devon

R. E. Webster, Dawlish, Devon

Richard Weeks, Amity Farm, Dawlish, Devon

Mr and Mrs F. W. West

Bryan Weston, Holcombe, Dawlish, Devon

Carolyn Whetman, Houndspool, Dawlish, Devon

Dinah Whitehead (née Farley), North Petherton, Somerset

Eddie Wiblin, Stonelands House, Dawlish, Devon

Derrick Willey, Dawlish, Devon

Bill, Bob and Joyce (née Ferrett), Nick Williams, Dawlish, Devon

Wendy and David Williams, Dawlish, Devon

Chris and Geraldine Woodwark, Dartmouth, Devon

Barbara A. Worley, Lanherne, Dawlish, Devon

Mrs Nicky E. Wright, Selgars, Exeter, Devon

Mrs Margaret Young, Dawlish, Devon

In order to include as many historic photographs as possible in this volume, a printed index is not included. However, the Community Histories are currently being indexed by Genuki. For further information and indexes to volumes in the series, please visit:

http://www.cs.ncl.ac.uk/genuki/DEV/indexingproject.html

THE BOOK OF DAWLISH

For details of any of these titles or if you are interested in writing your own community history, please contact: Community Histories Editor, Halsgrove House, Lower Moor Way, Tiverton Business Park, Tiverton, Devon EX16 6SS, England
e-mail: sales@halsgrove.com

A Dawlish donkey carriage, c.1865.